MW00714868

"*Where was this book when* *information and inspiratic* *anteed success!*"

Roy Saunderson,
President of the CAPS Southwest Ontario Chapter
London, Ontario, Canada

"*You can have two PhDs, been the CEO of a billion dollar company, won the national sales award six years in a row and none of it prepares you for the business of professional speaking. It is a business and calling like no other, and if it is calling to you there is finally a resource that will help you build it successfully.*

Blunt, practical, encouraging. Save yourself a lot of time, frustration and money start and build your career with this book!"

Ian Percy, CSP, Canadian Speaking Hall of Fame Member,
Author of *The 7 Secrets to a Life of Meaning*
Scottsdale, Arizona, USA

"*If you want to shorten your learning curve significantly and energize your speaking career, this is a must read of practical information related by those who have been there and done it!*"

Kit Grant, CSP, Canadian Speaking Hall of Fame Member,
Past World President & Chair of the International
Federation of Professional Speakers
Calgary, Alberta, Canada

"*Few things are as inspiring—and instructive—as being able to walk in the footsteps of those who have already made the journey to success.*"

Peter B. Legge LL.B (Hon) CSP, CPAE,
Canadian Speaking Hall of Fame Member
Burnaby, British Columbia, Canada

"*Cavett Robert, founder of NSA, advised aspiring speakers to shorten their learning curve by using (OPE), Other People's Experience. This book, filled with OPE, would make Cavett proud.*"

Jim Rhode, BSME, CSP,
National Speakers Association President (2002)
Phoenix, Arizona, USA

"*Today's competitive edge is accelerated learning.* Professionally Speaking Volume One *is designed to help all speakers hone their competitive edge and accelerate their learning.*"

Dr. Brad McRae,
Author of *The Seven Strategies of Master Negotiators*
Halifax, Nova Scotia, Canada

PROFESSIONALLY SPEAKING
VOLUME ONE

Belleville, Ontario, Canada

Professionally Speaking Volume One

ISBN: 1-55306-412-7

Cover Design by www.themarketingcentre.com

**For more information or
to order additional copies, please contact:**

caps@essencebookstore.com

Epic Press is an imprint of *Essence Publishing.*
For more information, contact:
44 Moira Street West, Belleville, Ontario, Canada K8P 1S3.
Phone: 1-800-238-6376. Fax: (613) 962-3055.
E-mail: info@essencegroup.com
Internet: www.essencegroup.com

Printed in Canada
by
Epic
Press

*This collection of personal success stories
is dedicated to people who make their living
as our teachers, coaches and mentors
—those committed individuals
who devote their passions and lives to making ours better.*

*They are the speakers and trainers who truly
make a difference.*

Francis J. Theriault
Project Leader

Welcome...

In this book, you'll be treated to some greatly inspiring stories from ordinary people who found ways to do extraordinary things with their lives. Our hope is that you will be encouraged and realize that you too can attain such outstanding personal accomplishments.

Please enjoy this book, share it with friends and let us know about your success stories. You can contact us at the CAPS, Toronto Chapter at **psbook@capstoronto.org**

Francis J. Theriault & Tim R. Paulsen
Project Co-ordinators

CAPS National President's Message

Valerie J. Cade Lee, CSP,
CAPS National President (2002)
Calgary, Alberta, Canada

Whether you are a speaker, are looking for a speaker or are interested in resources related to the speaking industry, our association represents hundreds of professional trainers, facilitators and keynote speakers from coast to coast.

CAPS is a professional association for people involved in the speaking business. Our members are versatile and diverse. They represent all aspects of the speaking business. All make their living, or part of their living, speaking to and/or working with groups as keynoters, trainers and facilitators.

CAPS is committed to building a better future for the professional speaking business in Canada. Our mission is to help our members succeed in their speaking businesses through learning partnerships, market development and professional accreditation. We also support international advancement of the speaking profession through our participation in and support for the National Speakers Association (USA) and the International Federation for Professional Speakers.

CAPS offers several categories of membership. Qualifications for the Professional and Associate categories are based on income, experience and willingness to abide by our *Code of Professional Ethics*. Affiliate memberships are open to bureaus, meeting planners, suppliers and people from other industry related groups.

CAPS is a learning community. Our highly rated annual convention is our flagship learning and community building opportunity. It's held in early December in Canadian cities reaching from Vancouver to Halifax.

Whatever your focus, your experience level or your stage of development, if you are a speaker, CAPS is the professional community that can help you discover what it will take to move your business to the next level.

Please visit our website at **www.canadianspeakers.org** for more information about joining our professional community, or attending a *CAPS Monthly Networking Meeting* or *Educational Event* near you.

NSA National President's Message

Jim Rhode, BSME, CSP
NSA National President (2002)

Jim sends his congratulations and offers the following words of encouragement to CAPS Toronto (Canadian Association of Professional Speakers) members:

> *"Cavett Robert, founder of NSA, advised aspiring speakers to shorten their learning curve by using (OPE),* Other People's Experiences. *This book, filled with OPEs, would make Cavett proud."*

Jim Rhode, BSME, CSP, National Speakers Association (USA) President (2002)

CAPS Toronto Chapter President's Message

Jean S. Sinden
CAPS Toronto Chapter President
(2002)
Oro Station, Ontario, Canada

STRENGTHENING OUR PROFESSION

As a career speaker, you owe it to yourself to be a member of the Canadian Association of Professional Speakers (CAPS). If you are located in the Greater Toronto Area, your best location to improve your business will be CAPS Toronto, which is the largest CAPS chapter in Canada.

We are professionals who make a living as Public Speakers, Trainers and Facilitators. The aim of CAPS Toronto is to provide our members with support, education, business building information, and high quality networking opportunities.

THE MAIN BENEFITS OF A CAPS TORONTO MEMBERSHIP ARE:

- networking with fellow professional speakers
- energizing your sales and marketing strategies
- sharpen your anecdotes with humor and receive the latest information on platform performance
- fine tuning your speeches, seminars and professional development workshops by watching and learning from our wealth of seasoned Toronto members and guest speakers from around the world
- preparing your content and delivery competency through our meetings, newsletter, tapes, website, lending library, membership directory, conferences, and specialized educational events.

At CAPS Toronto, we work hard to raise our profile and enhance our reputation in the industry (and in the media), we enjoy many opportunities to network with members and the members of other meetings industry organizations, such as Meeting Planners International (MPI), The Ontario Society of Training and Development (OSTD), The Canadian Society of Association Executives (CSAE) and many other local and national organizations.

Please visit our website at **www.capstoronto.org** for more information about attending a *CAPS Toronto Monthly Networking Meeting* or *Educational Event* soon, and about joining our professional community.

Table of Contents

Reference Section

Acknowledgements

THANKS TO CONTRIBUTORS AND THOSE WHO WORKED ON THIS PROJECT!

It wouldn't be enough to simply say thank you for a job well done. So, we'll print it now and say it often, since without your tremendous effort, care and consideration, this work could not exist. With your collective efforts, we hope this book will make a real difference in the reader's lives.

IMPORTANT KUDOS GOES TO:

Francis J. Theriault and Tim R. Paulsen for your team work and for your long-suffering, dedicated pursuit of this project, and for your many years of valued service to CAPS.

Gus Henne, Marketing Manager and Rikki-Anne McNaught, Acquisitions Editor for their commitment, talent and professionalism. In fact, absolutely everyone at *Essence Publishing* was accommodating and totally committed to this endeavor. People like these are a complement to the world of business.

Carol Clarke, of *Edit-Sharp Professional Writing and Editing Services.* Your talent is editing, your value is in your enthusiasm, but your special gift is coaching. All of the authors have remarked about how much they enjoyed working with you. You are a treasure.

Dean Jones and his staff at *The Marketing Centre*, whose marketing expertise and business savvy pulled the information together as only a seasoned, dedicated professional can do. Thanks Dean.

Purpose Statement

Why these authors, their content and why now? Why indeed? Our research has revealed that this book is exceptional; of 150 business and motivational samples, we found nothing comparable to the value found in this collaborative offering of career advice and business insights.

> *"Therefore, the goal of our book is to inform and inspire you, to add encouragement, to help you persevere in all your endeavors as a professional speaker. Whether you're a motivational or keynote speaker, a celebrity, trainer, facilitator, teacher, professor, the mentors in this book have been there and done it all."*

We want to share with you the trials and triumphs which await all of us when we dream and dare to make a difference in our world. Knowledge is a powerful liberator. It has been said that we have to learn from mistakes, but we don't have to make all of them ourselves. At every opportunity, we can and should learn from each other.

We wish to inspire you because people who make significant social, spiritual, political or economic contributions often say it's because they feel "called" to a life of service through leadership. And everyone, without fail, will recall the teachers, coaches and mentors who have invested in our lives and made a genuine and lasting difference. Above all else, the authors of this book want to invest themselves in your life by offering their experiences and positive energy.

Introduction to CAPS

(Canadian Association of Professional Speakers)

CAPS/NSA SHARED HISTORY AND VISION

In 1973, NSA's (National Speakers Association) founder, Cavett Robert, CSP, CPAE, had a vision for an organization where professional speakers could convene to improve their presentations, exchange ideas and share experiences. He also felt that everyone involved in the profession of speaking would benefit from growing the number and quality of professional speakers.

Before we can tell you about CAPS (Canadian Association of Professional Speakers), we must mention the forerunner organization, which was started in 1986 in Toronto and was known as OSA (Ontario Speakers Association). OSA was an international chapter of NSA, as were similar professional associations in other provinces, which were all incorporated as a Canadian National Organization by the name of CAPS in 1977 .

At that time, it also made sense to create the IFPS (International Federation for Professional Speakers), and so it was done, with Canada's leadership, the United States, Australia and New Zealand—and shortly thereafter joined by Europe—formed the first member countries of the IFPS in 1997. Today, all of these organizations (with their 5,000 plus members) enjoy international networking, education and speaking opportunities.

CAPS CODE OF PROFESSIONAL ETHICS

To establish and maintain public confidence in the professionalism, honesty, ability and integrity of the professional speaker is fundamental to the future success of the association, its members, and the profession of speaking.

To this end, members of the association have adopted and, as a condition of membership, subscribed to a *Code of Professional Ethics*. By doing so, members give notice that they recognize the vital need to preserve and encourage fair and equitable practices among all who are engaged in the profession of speaking.

CAPS VISION AND MISSION STATEMENTS

The CAPS Vision is to be recognized as: Creating the future for the professional speaking business in Canada.

The CAPS Mission is to help members succeed in their speaking business through: Learning Partnerships, Market Development and Professional Recognition… to add value for the clients we serve.

CAPS EIGHT COMPETENCY AREAS OF FOCUS

- Authorship and Product Development
- Managing the Business
- Platform Mechanics
- Presenting and Performing
- Professional Awareness
- Professional Relationships
- Sales and Marketing
- Topic Development

CAPS/NSA SHARED ACCREDITATIONS (CSP, CPAE, HoF)

CSP—*Certified Speaking Professional* is the highest earned designation for professional achievement. Earned through a combination of high standards in: association, education, performance and business management.

CPAE—*Council of Peers Award of Excellence*

HoF—*Canadian Speaking Hall of Fame*

Both the CPAE and the HoF designations are awarded annually—through the evaluation of existing CPAE and HoF members—to professional speakers who demonstrate platform excellence and complete professionalism.

Susan Armstrong

Training & Development

Barrie, ON Canada
Phone: 705-734-2199
Toll Free: 877-368-9200
E-mail: sue.gwil@rogers.com.

SUSAN ARMSTRONG *is a Training and Development Professional specializing in Sales and Customer Service. For over 20 years, Susan has been working in Sales and Sales Management roles in the Hospitality, Telecommunications and Financial industries. During this time, she has developed a high level of skill in a Sales capacity, winning many Top Sales and Top Sales Management awards. Susan has been designing and facilitating Sales and Customer Service training for the last ten years, working to improve the performance and productivity of professionals in a wide range of industries. Her interactive and entertaining workshops and training sessions have been described as "the best I have ever attended" by numerous participants.*

In keynote speeches, Susan specializes in Motivation. Speaking for audiences ranging from 30 people to over 1500, she is able to captivate and inspire her audience. Her personal story, which encompasses some very extraordinary events, has been featured on both the Discovery Channel and the Life Network.

• How I Got Started

Just today, I was reminded of how I got launched into this business. I read an article about stress in the workplace. It had one of those quizzes; you know, 10 questions:

"Do you ever take work home with you on holidays, evenings, and weekends?" Answer: Doesn't everyone?

"Do you work more than 45 hours per week?" Answer: I run my own business. Isn't 45 hours per week *part time?*

"Do you like to do everything perfectly or not at all?" (I don't see the outcome of this quiz) Answer: To repeat, I run my own business.

"Do you have a tough time relaxing when you're not working?" O.K., now they must be kidding! Answer: R-E-L-A-X? I tried it once and it didn't fit my schedule.

The greatest achievement of the human spirit is to live up to one's opportunities and make the most of one's resources. Marquis De Vauvenargues

---

Anyway, you get the drift. The outcome was, as you have probably guessed, that in fact I do have stress at work. I scored 9 out of 10 stress points, which indicated, according to the Ph.D. who wrote the article, that I am a workaholic. The only answer I was penalized for was my response to: "Do you get impatient with people who talk about their life outside of work?" Answer: On the contrary! I aspire to one of those "life outside of work" things—as soon as I can figure out what it is. (Maybe I should do a "needs" assessment?)

Workaholic. Imagine! Just because I'm more comfortable in a hotel room than my own bedroom doesn't mean I'm a workaholic. OK, I was a little concerned when recently I found myself saying goodbye to my lovely hotel bed and hugging the concierge staff. But doesn't everyone cry when they leave much loved and trusted friends? I mean, where do you draw the line between workaholic and hobbyist? That's right, hobbyist. Personally, I consider myself a hobbyist because that's what my work is—my hobby.

Unfortunately, that hasn't always been the case. I had spent many years putting in 60 hours a week, wondering if there wasn't more to life—that is, until my father died. And then I realized that there was definitely more to life. Suddenly, I wanted to experience more. Fortunately, my father left me a small inheritance, enough to buy myself a new outlook. I took six weeks off work and set out to discover how to complete myself. As I sat and contemplated what I might like to do in my new life, I couldn't help but think about my father. Here was a very smart man who died never doing any of the things he wanted to do. By his own admission he was scared. His dreams had been foiled by fear.

I dread success. To have succeeded is to have finished one's business on earth, like the male spider, who is killed by the female the moment he has succeeded in courtship. I like a state of continual becoming, with a goal in front and not behind.

George Bernard Shaw

During my six weeks of reflection, I attended some support groups that dealt with grief, self-esteem (my father's death hit me hard), and even took in some meetings about career planning. Heck, I even went so far as to speak at one of the self-esteem meetings. It wasn't a new thing for me. I had been speaking at small gatherings for 5 years. Women's groups mostly. It made me feel good to be able to help people. There was no money involved, just my time and the sense of satisfaction I received. During a meeting, I mentioned that my father had passed away and commented on the effect it had on my self-esteem. Afterwards, a woman approached me. She expressed her appreciation for my honesty and said that I had moved her to take steps to recover her own sense of esteem. That was great. I felt really good! She went on to say that I was in the right job and she hoped she would have the opportunity to hear me speak again. Huh! Wasn't that nice? And this wasn't even my job! I just did it because it made me feel good. Now what was that saying about "Do what you love and the money will follow"?

• My Biggest Mistake

Absolutely without a doubt, wearing a dress to a very important keynote. It was a fancy occasion. You know: Hollywood lights and sound, a guy following me around to check my voice levels, and making sure I looked 29 under the lights. And, of course wiring me up for sound.

During rehearsal, we did the run-through of my talk to make sure the lights, sound, and technology worked. All went well. The next day, I was dressed for success! Lovely plum dress with matching jacket. Understated jewelry. Everything was perfect! Down I went to the ballroom in the hotel and here comes my sound guy Mike looking at me strangely. "Where are you going to put the pack?" he asks. *Oh*, I think to myself. "I know! I'll hook it to the inside of the waistband of my pantyhose! That'll work." So Mike and I trot off to the ladies' restroom and I partially undress (a humiliating experience in itself) and voila! I'm wired.

A life spent making mistakes is not only more honorable, but more useful than a life spent doing nothing. George Bernard Shaw

---

Finally, it's my turn on stage and a big academy award voice booms "And now, please help me welcome Ms. Susan Armstrong!" Applause. I begin my talk; everything is going beautifully. That is, until the microphone pack unhooked itself from the waistband of my pantyhose and started to work its way down my leg. Now, here I am, on stage, a very important performance, and I have a microphone pack sliding down my leg. To slow its progress, reverse it if possible, I began a series of convulsive twists and rapid squats—the whole time carrying on with my speech. The wide-eyed audience must have assumed I had some embarrassing bladder urgency. And if you really need a visual, I still have the videotape. There was very big key learning here.

Biggest mistake on the platform: Taking myself too seriously.

Courage is fear that has said its prayers.
Karle Wilson Baker

• My Best Success

Helping others. That's what I do. I help people improve their personal and working lives. In my opinion, that's what makes me successful.

I have learned that success is to be measured not so much by the position that one has reached in life as by the obstacles which he has overcome while trying to succeed.
Booker T. Washington

• What I Would Do Over

I would have joined CAPS sooner and not have been so scared to ask for help. I would have trusted in myself and in my instincts a little more. It's true what they say. With age comes wisdom, and may I add… self-worth. That's why I'm so grateful for our industry. Bring on 50! I'm ready. My father would have been proud.

Peter Urs Bender, CSP, HoF

FOREMOST AUTHORITY ON

Presentations Skills

Bestselling author on topics of Leadership, Marketing & Presentations

Toronto, ON Canada
Phone: 416-490-6690
Fax: 416-490-0375
E-mail: Bender@PeterUrsBender.com
Web: **www.Bender.ca**

PETER URS BENDER: *Born in Switzerland, Peter comes from an accounting and banking background. He was expected to follow in the family footsteps, but he was a total failure in school. (Years later, when one of his wife's children was tested for suspected dyslexia, he discovered to his astonishment he himself had the learning disability that makes reading, and hence learning, very difficult.)*

In Toronto, when he did well as a salesman, his company insisted he take a Dale Carnegie course. He resisted, "Why do I need to take a sales course?" He may have gone for the wrong reasons but found it to be be a life changing opportunity.

Bender also learned something else: that to be successful he had to learn to present. So he joined a Toronto group similar to Toastmasters.

He was uptight at first, but he persevered and gradually he became better—good enough, in fact, to begin teaching at Ryerson University in downtown Toronto.

Today, he has transformed that Teaching and Sales experience into four best sellers:
- Secrets of Power Presentations
- Leadership from Within

- Secrets of Power Marketing
- Secrets of Face to Face Communication

He has just published another book: Gutfeeling.

His first book, Secrets of Power Presentations, *pragmatically recapped everything he had learned from his speaking club, sales presenting, and teaching experience. The book became a bestseller in Canada, then went on to become an international bestseller, translated into ten languages, and still a best-selling book a decade later.*

After the success of Presentations, *Bender's two other books found a ready market with a well-known Canadian publisher, and are following the same bestseller path.*

• How I Got Started

My introduction to the speaking profession began when as a salesman I realized that to be really successful I had to know how to present. So I did what many young men before me had done. I joined a Toronto group very similar to Toastmasters. We met in the Albany Club twice a month. I remember being absolutely terrified. The last thing I wanted to do was stand up in public and make a spectacle of myself. In my book *Secrets of Power Presentations*, I say that the three worst fears of anyone are: 1) speaking in public, 2) dying, and 3) speaking and dying in public. That was more than true for me!

Your past was perfect to get you where you are today. Peter Urs Bender

---

The meetings came prepackaged with meals but I could never enjoy them because I was too sick with worry. If I was 19th in a list of 20 speakers, I heard none of the previous presentations. I was too uptight. But I knew I had to persist, and I did. Gradually I got better—

good enough, in fact, to be asked to teach a sales course at Ryerson University. Imagine me a teacher when, with my dyslexia. I couldn't spell and had great difficulty in reading!

• **My Biggest Mistake**

When I first started giving courses, I was literally only one chapter ahead of the class. I used to force myself to read the course books chapter by chapter, until I was sure I had mastered the material well enough to present it to my students. Of course, I had plenty of field sales experience to rely on, but teaching a course with texts, and expounding on points academically was foreign to me. It was great training, though. I eventually wound up teaching four different part-time courses at Ryerson for almost fifteen years. In a sense, all I know, and all I put into practice on the platform today, I learned from teaching.

If we do what we always done, we get what we always gotten. Peter Urs Bender

---

• **My Best Success**

I knew many people who had this fear of public speaking. I also knew that to succeed in business it was vital to be able to communicate your ideas. In the 80s, to be different from other speakers, you had to have a book. So I decided to write one on presenting. I tried to recap everything I had learned from my speaking club, my sales presenting, and my teaching. Although I tried repeatedly to find a publisher, I could not. I decided to self-publish.

It was the right move. My book became a bestseller in a field where many books already existed, but none as pragmatic as mine. I deliberately kept my writing style simple and down-to-earth, (mainly because I couldn't do anything fancy) and it won me international support. That was when I realized it was possible to turn a handicap into an asset. The book became a bestseller in Canada, and then went on to become an international bestseller. It was translated into more than ten languages, and is still a best-selling book a decade later. It has just been republished in a jubilee edition, revised and updated as a result of the new technology available to presenters.

> ## You cannot—not market.
> Peter Urs Bender

• What I Would Do Over

I learned three major lessons from my experiences at becoming a speaker. First, to everything there is a system. With a system, even a person of mediocre talent can become a success. Second, persistence is critical. I like to say that you haven't failed until you've fallen down and don't get up. I also learned that the second time you try something, it gets easier. So, I decided to try another book. The third important secret is that in writing or preparing any book, it pays to have expert assistance. That's especially true for someone like myself for whom English is a second language, and dyslexia a constant presence.

At the risk of sounding old-fashioned, I discovered that an assistant must be of good character, energetic (that is, he or she must work hard), and business oriented. If these sound like old-fashioned virtues, they are. But they are critical to a successful writing partnership. All the ideas that had been boiling around in my mind while I was writing *Secrets of Power Presentations*, as well as my fascination with the qualities that make a good leader led me to my second book, *Leadership from Within*. For this project I had the assistance of Eric Hellman, an experienced writer and editor. His contribution enabled me to fine-tune my thoughts quickly, and he kept the project on track through the difficult first writing phase. He also made major contributions to the structure of the book. While the thoughts and ideas in it are mine, the expression of them became much more sophisticated in Eric's hands.

The smarter I work, the luckier I get.

Peter Urs Bender

The same pattern held true for my third and fourth books, *Secrets of Power Marketing* and *Secrets of Face-to-Face Communication*. With both of these books, the original manuscript came from my co-authors, George Torok in Marketing, and Dr. Robert Tracz in Communication. Both books were worked over several times so that in the end they became true co-authored publications—books that genuinely reflected the points of view of all participants.

Do not read your speech—read your audience.

Peter Urs Bender

My fifth and newly published book, *Gutfeeling*, however, was a true collaboration with my assistant George Hancocks. Right from the beginning I gave George a list of chapter titles. He started writing. Then he printed out. I revised and adjusted. Then he began adding chapter titles himself and would "interview" me about what I wanted to say. He would write it down, revise it, and we would discuss it. Sometimes he would write something on his own and ask me what I thought. We bounced ideas and words back and forth right up until the final type was set. And all along we simplified, simplified,

simplified. The whole experience became what I have always imagined a "co-authorship" could be. It was an energizing experience and the lesson is clear. If I can do it, anyone can—as long as the right people are involved.

Anne Thornley-Brown

Creativity
Balance
Spirituality

The Training Oasis, Inc.

Phone: 905-887-5224.
E-mail: anne@thetrainingoasis.com.
Web: **www.thetrainingoasis.com**

ANNE THORNLEY-BROWN *is a Jamaican-born, Professional Speaker, Instructional Designer and Facilitator. She has over 20 years of experience in a variety of industries including wireless communications, banking, transportation, film and television, and the non-profit sector. Anne has delivered seminars and speeches to executives and professionals in Canada, Malaysia, Singapore, India, and Jamaica. She has an M.B.A. from York University in Toronto and an MSW from the University of Illinois (Urbana-Champaign campus). Anne has been on executive teams and boards for CAPS—Toronto, the MBA Women's Association, and the Ontario Society for Training and Development.*

Anne's style of presentation is upbeat, energetic and creative. She uses music, props, energizers and themes to "spice up" her speeches and training sessions. As one client advised "If you want boring, don't call Anne". What is unique about Anne's approach is that her work is the perfect blend of solid business acumen and creativity. Anne draws her creativity from her experience as a professional actress and writer. You'll recognize Anne as Spike's counselor on the international Emmy award winning TV series, "Degrassi Junior High". Anne's other television credits include "Doc", starring Billy Ray

Cyrus, the Mary Higgins Clark Mysteries, and Louis Del Grande's made-for-TV movie, Sanity Clause.

Oasis = a place of calm in the midst of turbulence

Anne is the founder and president of The Training Oasis, Inc., a management consulting firm for organizations experiencing change, growth and competitive pressures. The "out of the box" strategies of The Training Oasis, Inc. help organizations survive, thrive and grow in a turbulent economy. The services of The Training Oasis, Inc. include the facilitation of executive meetings, executive retreats, team-building sessions, and accelerated learning programmes.

• How I Got Started

I guess I have always had "the gift of the gab". When I was a child, my parents used to tell me that I had been vaccinated with a gramophone needle. I first realized the extent of my gift when I aced an impromptu speech in grade eight English class at good old Montreal High. I was asked to speak for 3 minutes about make-up and I could have gone on for hours.

Nothing great was ever achieved without enthusiasm.

Emerson

Throughout high school, I was involved in the debating and drama clubs. The first speaking I did for large audiences was when I was a teenager. I am a born-again Christian and I had many opportunities to speak at church youth groups, as a camp counselor at Frontier Lodge Christian Youth Camp and as a Sunday School teacher at People's

Church. Little did I know that I would one day be earning my living as a professional speaker.

I began speaking professionally, after I co-authored the book, *West Indians in Toronto: Implications for Helping Professionals* for the Family Service Association of Metro Toronto. This was one of my first jobs after I graduated with my social work degree. As part of this job, I designed and co-facilitated diversity workshops for the agency staff. After the book was released, I began to receive invitations to speak about diversity for social agencies, hospitals and educational institutions.

After working as a professional counselor for 7 years, the transition to speaking for business audiences did not come easily. One of the realities for which I was inadequately prepared was discrimination on the basis of race and sex. I naively expected doors to open for me just because I had the requisite experience and education. This was not to be the case. It took hard work, persistence and the ability to bounce back from rejection to break through the barriers I faced. I thank professional speakers and trainers like Warren Evans, Gail Friedlander and Des Mackle for their no-holds barred and candid feedback and support. I followed Warren's advice to get some solid business experience under my belt. It eventually paid off. After a stint in commercial credit at The Toronto-Dominion Bank, the doors slowly began to open for me to become involved in training and speaking on a full-time basis.

─────────────

The brighter you are, the more you have to learn.

Ralph Waldo Emerson

─────────────

The first full-time training position I held was a contract with Theatre Direct Canada. I wrote *A Resource Guide on Sexual Coercion for Educators* and facilitated train-the-trainer workshops to accompany the Dora Mavor Moore award winning play *Thin Ice*. Then, I obtained management development specialist positions for 2 corporations.

After spending a number of years in the corporate sector designing and delivering seminars for executives and managers, I made the transition to speaking and training on an independent basis. This was another difficult transition. Initially, I did freelance work for other training and consulting firms. I also designed, advertised and facilitated "Career Makeover" workshops at The McGill Club and The Elmwood Club in Toronto. It was hard work and the audiences were small but appreciative. There were many ups and downs but gradually I was able to develop a client base and grow my business.

It matters not how long we live, but how.

Bailey

• My Biggest Mistake

There have been many but I guess the biggest was following advice from a popular seminar company about the need to review your credentials with an audience. I did this in front of several customer service management groups and I got killed. Most of the managers had, at best, a high school diploma. Stressing my academic qualifications made me seem arrogant and alienated my audience. It was not easy to re-gain rapport with them.

Another huge mistake was to spend $10,000 to sponsor a professional association for 2 years. It produced no business and the money I spent would have been put to better use publishing a book, developing a video and obtaining a shopping cart system so that I could sell products from my web site.

• My Best Success

My best success has come from having friends and colleagues to provide me with prayer, support and guidance through the ups and downs of building a speaking business. There were a number of occasions on which business just seemed to dry up and I found myself facing financial pressure. When members of my friends, colleagues and members of my church group for entrepreneurs have spent time with me in prayer, I experienced incredible breakthroughs such as multiple engagements with large corporations and the opportunity to travel to Asia on a professional engagement. At the time of writing, I am preparing to head over to Asia for the 5th time in 2 years.

Many receive advice, only the wise profit by it.

Syrus

My company, The Training Oasis, Inc. and its web site, www.thetrainingoasis.com, have been profiled in a number of publications including *Computing Canada*, *Professional Administrator* magazine, *Sympatico Netlife*, *ASTD's Technical Training* magazine, *Accelerated Learning Network News*, and *The Training Report* newspaper. Our web site, a virtual oasis, been consistently rated in the top 2 in Compass, The Discian Group's ranking of over 100 training related sites around the globe. The Training Oasis, Inc.'s virtual newsletters, *Executive Enclave* and *Spice of the Month*, are popular with executives and trainers around the globe. Our clients have included Wurth Canada, Novo Nordisk Canada, IKEA, Manulife Financial, CGU Group Canada, Ltd., Ingram Micro, Telus Mobility (formerly Clearnet PCS Inc.), IBM, and Bell Mobility. Our Asian clients have included OCBC Bank, Penang Port and Permodalan Nasional Berhad in Malaysia. Not bad for someone who came to Canada as a toddler from a small island in the sun so many years ago.

• **What I Would Do Over**

If I had it all to do over again, knowing then what I know now, I would do many things differently. First of all, I would have gone out on my own earlier. It was a huge risk but the pay off has been tremendous. It has made it possible for me to have interesting assignments, travel to exotic locations and experience greater balance between the personal and professional areas of my life.

Another thing that I would have done was to build a larger financial cushion before heading out on my own. The conventional wisdom has been that individuals should have enough money to cover 6 months worth of living expenses before launching a business. Given the volatile economy, one years worth of reserves would have been advisable. At times, due to financial pressures, I have caved in and allowed clients to drastically hammer me down on my rate. This has come back to haunt me on more than one occasion. I have also ended up taking assignments that were not ideal for my skill set or personality because I needed the money.

The other thing that I should have done earlier is target the executive market. When I launched The Training Oasis, I realized that I had a choice between marketing train the trainer services or services for executives. Since I already had an extensive network among trainers, this market seemed like an easier sell. Unfortunately, I found myself spinning my wheels as, at times, trainers did not have the decision-making authority or budget to secure my services.

No person should part with their individuality and become that of another. Channing

---

If I had it to do all over again, I would have launched my web site earlier. It has helped me build a network in every corner of the globe. I would also have invested in professionally designed logo, business cards and stationary before I went out on my own. For a long time, my nervousness about the quality of my collateral material made me hesitant to approach executive audiences. As it turned out, I worried needlessly and let this undermine my confidence. Since upgrading my collateral and promotional material, no executive has ever asked me for a business card or brochure.

As I reflect on my career, I think my biggest blind spot has been to assume that strategies that work for "every body else" would work for me. Each individual is unique. God has a special path for each of us. While we can learn from one another, there is no recipe for success. At times I have approached my career as a never-ending search for magic answers and formulas. This has lead to frustration and caused me to go down blind alleys. It has taken me a long time to gain confidence but I have finally learned to stop trying to be a carbon copy of other people who have "made it". The Lord has given me the courage to be myself and helped me to gradually find my audience.

Nothing is so contagious as enthusiasm; it moves stones, it tames brutes. Enthusiasm is the genius of sincerity and truth accomplishes no victories without it. Bulwer-Lytton

---

Performance Advantage, Inc.

Brampton, ON Canada
Phone: 905-459-2496
Toll Free: 888-650-9022
Fax: 905-459-1045
E-mail: brian@bdalzell.com
Web: **www.bdalzell.com**

Brian G. Dalzell

BRIAN G. DALZELL *is a Speaker, Facilitator and Consultant with over 25 years of business experience, working in and with many industries at the executive level. He has spoken to audiences in North and South America as well as Australia, Britain, Hong Kong, Japan, Korea and The Peoples Republic of China.*

He is Past President of the Canadian Association of Professional Speakers and is a current member of the International Federation for Professional Speakers.

Brian has been referred to as a "Dynamic, humorous & insightful speaker who brings understanding to relevant business & personal issues". He specializes in Sales, Performance Management, Strategic Planning and Executive retreats.

He is president of The Performance Advantage Inc. a successful consulting firm providing a broad spectrum of services to organizations ranging in size from Multi-Nationals to Independent Business as well as the public sector, unions and not-for-profit. His personal and corporate mission is to "Help people and organizations achieve their full potential—through meaningful and lasting transformation".

• How I Got Started

After 15 years in several organizations, and having become the head of Training and Development for one of Canada's largest banks, it became clear that I just was no longer having fun. So, in 1990 I left the bank to start my own training business. After all, I could train, had helped people and organizations grow, and I could sell my ideas and myself fairly well. What more could I need?

Only you can do it, but you don't have to do it alone. Brian Dalzell

---

The first year could have been a complete disaster if not for the fact that a friend, Judy Winestone, had given me a lead. I followed up and got the project, which spanned several months. During that time I made a huge number of calls, but with few contacts and limited success. It seems there was a recession taking place, a detail I had failed to take into account.

During this time, I developed a new relationship with our mailman. I could see our mailbox from my office and could tell you when he was running late (and by how many minutes) while I waited to see if he had a cheque for me. There were always lots of envelopes—usually bills and junk mail that I quickly cast aside looking for the elusive envelope with the corporate logo in the top left hand corner. I still sort mail this way 12 years later. If any of the neighbours were watching, I'm sure they wondered why I'd pump my fist and do a little dance when that special logo appeared. That hasn't changed.

• My Biggest Mistake

My biggest mistake getting started was in the area of marketing, yet I knew this stuff. In fact, I teach it to my clients. I knew major corporations and how they worked, or at least I thought I did. I didn't, however, pay a lot of attention to *how they did business with people on the outside.* On that front, they were a lot less friendly. There was no way you could work for them if you weren't in their budget description. Their sales cycle was 12 to 24 months. I had a monthly mortgage, and with a growing family, weekly groceries; the cycles just weren't meshing.

Trees can't run, rocks can't fly and rivers just flow without purpose. People do the best they can with what they have and who they are. Brian Dalzell

---

Like any intelligent person in a financial crisis, I overreacted and slid way down market to small independent businesses. Now these people needed help, thought I was brilliant, but they didn't have any money. They used phrases like "You've got to be (expletive) kidding!" when I told them what my fees were, and back then… they were low.

The good news about first-hand learning is that it makes for great stories in sales courses on what *not* to do. It also meant there was really only one area left for me to try—the *mid-market* business. These organizations had a need, had money to spend and the sales cycle was 6–12 months (sometimes shorter), which was getting a lot closer to the cycle I had for food and shelter. Life was good and so was business. Or was it, business was good; ergo, so was life! It's funny how those two things seem to get linked together.

• My Best Success

Once the hunger went away and the hole in the roof got fixed, I wanted to grow my business and started looking around for like-minded souls. It was then that I met Ian Cook who introduced me to CAPS (at that time, The Ontario Speakers Association). He encouraged me to come out to meetings and get to know people. I did, and reaped unexpected benefits. Not only did I meet some dynamic individuals, I got to learn about myself and what I needed to do to take my business to the next level.

Over the years, I have been coached and mentored by some great people including David Sweet, Warren Evans (CSP, HoF) and Alan Giles along with several others who were all helpful. I remember one evening in particular when I was feeling a little down and I asked several of them what I assumed was a somewhat dumb question: "How do you know if you're successful?" The questions they asked helped, but one question asked by Alan Simmons (CSP, HoF) especially hit home. He asked, "Are you making a difference?" I wasn't sure at the time, but since then, I have pursued the answer with every client. Not through the "happy sheets" at the end of a session, but later when they are back on the job applying what we delivered, I ask: "How did we help you or your organization to better achieve your goals?" Their answers tell me when I've made a difference.

Fear is the gatekeeper to our new realities.
Brian Dalzell

Our success has been a blend of hard work, quality services and much appreciated references from some great friends and associates. For years, Rick Van Allen has introduced me to people who might be a good fit for me the type of services we provide. His caring has significantly contributed to our success and has definitely reduced the time needed to find new work and improve our closing ratios. Asking people who care about you and who want to see you successful, "Who do you know that might need my services?" is one of the most effective tools you can employ to build your business.

Beliefs are like Boxes. We can either build Barriers or Bridges. Brian Dalzell

---

• What I Would Do Over

My advice to others starting out:

1) Do more networking before you quit your day job.

2) Ask more of your friends sooner for referrals.

3) Have more confidence to raise your fees when you get busy. There seems to be a perception that if you don't charge very much, you can't be very good, but if you do charge more you must be good. Go figure.

Our biggest gains in learning come from our greatest losses in life. Brian Dalzell

---

I wish all those who read this book the joy, success and good friendships this great business of professional speaking has brought into my life. Good luck and God Bless.

Peter de Jager

Managing Change & Technology

Brampton, ON Canada
Phone: 905-792-8706
Fax: 905-792-9818
E-mail: Pdejager@technobility.com
Web: www.technobility.com

PETER DE JAGER *is a Speaker, Consultant, Writer on issues relating to the Management of our Future—technological and otherwise. He's published hundreds of articles on Creativity, Change, the Future and Technology. His articles have appeared in* The Washington Post, The Wall Street Journal *and* Scientific American.

He publishes three items of special interest which are all free, e-mailed and available on his Web site:
- *A Journal on Managing Change & Technology*
- *A Collection of Tips, Tricks and Thoughts called* **Event Horizons**
- **Truth Picks** *…mini essays prompted by famous quotes.*

He's spoken in more than 30 countries. His audiences include the World Economic Forum, The World Bank and The Bank for International Settlements. He's appeared on CBC, ABC, *"Dateline", "Nightline" and "Crossfire" to name a handful of some 2,000+ media appearances.*

His presentations are provocative. He attacks, with humor of course, the myths surrounding our understanding of both the Change process and Technology. The only objective of his presentations is to provide actionable items which help immediately with both the man-

agement of change and the ability to create a desirable future.

His sessions are interactive, fun, challenging and irreverent to mistaken ideas. He writes regular columns for CIO Magazine *and* Computing Canada, *and has just published a collection of writings entitled* Truth Picks.

• How I Got Started

In the early 1980s I attended numerous conferences as a part of my role as the manager responsible for the introduction of Personal Computers into the corporate business environment. Most of the industry speakers I watched, and listened to, repeated a single statement as they flashed a slide onto the screen. That statement stuck in my mind. Here it is for your edification and grand amusement (I've added an editorial comment to close it off!):

> "I know you can't read this, but…"
> *I'm going to put it up anyway… just to annoy you.*

The slide they then show would contain one, sometimes all, of the following cardinal sins of presenting:

a) Words in yellow on a white background, or black on a dark blue background.

b) So much detail it was impossible to read.

I was struck by two different thoughts. First, if the purpose of showing a slide in a presentation is to communicate information, then it is an act of madness to display a slide you know in advance the audience cannot read.

It's a blatant display of the old joke… Doctor, Doctor, it hurts when I do this…

Speak to me from the heart; I'll use mine to listen. PdJ

The second thought was that if I did nothing else but avoid the necessity of ever saying "I know you can't read this but…" to an audience, then I would do a better job than 9 out of 10 speakers.

This, more than any other factor, is why I began speaking in the first place. The reason I continue speaking is that there is no other more effective means of influencing people than by communicating plainly, and with passion from the heart, about what you believe in.

• My Biggest Mistake

It's nearly impossible to fix a problem when it falls beneath the radar of both yourself and the audience. Without a clue that something is going wrong, you naturally assume that everything is going right.

I'd been speaking for years, had given hundreds of talks, and was making the same peculiar mistake over and over again without being aware of it.

In hindsight it was costing me at least .5-1 points on the evaluation sheets, maybe more. Yet even if you'd asked the audience why they were marking me down, they'd be unable to tell you. The mistake is "oh, so subtle", but has a huge impact on your relationship with the audience, and therefore on your performance.

The tallest mountains lean up against the deepest valleys. PdJ

How did I become aware of my perpetual flub? I'd just finished sharing the platform with Warren Evans in Steamboat Springs, CO and we were hoisting a jar to our success. He mentioned that occasionally I "stepped on my own lines".

I hadn't heard that phrase before and asked for an explanation. He explained that sometimes when the audience found something I said to be funny, they'd start laughing. But before they'd finished enjoying the moment, I'd continue with what I had to say.

This problem is related to that nebulous thing called "timing" and how closely you pay attention to the audience. I was obviously aware they were laughing. How could I miss it? But they'd paid for a talk, and a talk they were going to get. My mistake.

What did I learn from all this? Trampling on the laughter of an audience isn't the way to endear them to you. If they find something you said funny, let them enjoy it, let them laugh, absolutely nothing you have to say is more important than the laughter of your listeners.

• My Best Success

I speak to communicate ideas, but any success I have had in this area didn't come from the podium, it came from my fingertips.

If our stock in trade is ideas, then writing is one of the best kept trade secrets. Putting ideas down on paper for an unseen audience is the best way to organize our thoughts.

The experience of others is knowledge awaiting harvest. PdJ

When we're in front of an audience, what we say and how we say it is important. Coming up with the perfect line while in the limelight is possible, but it's doing it the hard way.

At our desk, we have the time, to play and toy with the timing and tone of a phrase. Getting it right on paper is less painful than getting it wrong on stage.

If a speaker deals in ideas, then articles become the source and finishing school for those ideas. Most of my success as a speaker I attribute directly to published articles that laid the groundwork for my presence on the stage.

Writing, not stage craft, is what gets us to the podium… then and only then do we get the chance to articulate our thoughts in front of a live audience. As speakers we have two tools to success, the pen and the podium.

• What I Would Do Over

The mistakes I've made, there were a few, were all the mistakes of growth and learning a new skill. They were as necessary as breathing. Except for one…

If I were starting over? I would start sooner. Speaking is ultimately the most fun you can have, in front of an audience, with your clothes on.

CANADIAN ASSOCIATION OF PROFESSIONAL SPEAKERS

CAPS

PROFESSIONAL TRAINERS,
FACILITATORS AND KEYNOTERS

Service Excellence Group, Inc.

Georgetown, ON Canada
Phone: 905-877-0624
Fax: 905-877-1681
E-mail: seg@wevans.com
Web: **www.wevans.com**

Warren Evans, CSP, HoF

WARREN EVANS *is President of* **The Service Excellence Group Inc.** *SEG is a management-consulting firm founded in 1977, with extensive corporate career roots in the areas of sales and marketing. They're known for their strategy work and for guiding change-implementation projects based on their Service Management models.*

Today, SEG's focus is on Trends Analysis and Strategy Work. Current research revolves around looking at how major trends interact with each other, in order to determine how they are most likely to unfold. Often running against conventional wisdom, this "trends blending" approach has allowed SEC to correctly call everything from organizational issues, stock market swings, real-estate values, and election results. They work with clients of every size and from every sector; including economic development entities from Scotland, Persian Gulf and Yukon. In fact, his firm has now served clients in a dozen countries on five continents.

Warren served for seven years on the Executive Council of the 165,000 member International Federation for Training and Development Organizations; was Chairman of the 5,000 member International Federation for Professional Speakers, and his articles have been published in professional journals around the world.

As a member of Mensa, various Societies for Training and Development and Professional Speakers Associations, Warren has been recognized with their highest earned designations including CSP (Certified Speaking Professional) and HoF (Hall of Fame Inductee).

• How I Got Started

I WANTED TO MAKE A DIFFERENCE

Like most people who have been doing this as long as I have (25 years), I found myself more in the speaking business than following a master plan to become a professional speaker.

My relatively short corporate career was in the sales and marketing trenches. By fluke of circumstance, both the major companies I worked for sold systems across the entire spectrum of organizations, so I had to learn how a wide variety of businesses functioned and the issues they faced.

You got great promotional material; it's word of mouth that's killing you. The CAPS Pool PEG

In the late '70s I launched a consulting business, which offered turn-around work for small organizations. Along the way, I acquired a silent interest in a company that imported packaged training products. By a long, convoluted story I ended up owning all of the company. It seemed a natural fit with our work activities and quickly became our core business.

I had a great advantage in the training business, which was that all of my previous exposure to corporate training was on the receiving end. That gave me a strong sense (or at least some strong opinions) of what was wrong with the training and most of it, and what ought to be done.

My new attitude and approach taught me that if you have genuine experience to draw on, your own instincts are just as valuable as conventional wisdom. However, to be successful, I needed to connect with that portion of the market that resonated with my own philosophy.

• My Biggest Mistake

NOT BEING DISTINCTIVE AND SPECIALIZED

Initially, I did some public seminars, which my good friend Kit Grant calls the "printing and postage business". In fact, I vividly recall Kit and I partnering on a series of seminars, and losing our financial shirts. We sat down and I told him the bad news, asking if he wanted to see the accounting records. He said "No, spare me the gory details, just tell me what I owe you." I did, and he pulled out his cheque book. I learned there are some first class people in this business, people that anyone would be privileged to call their friend.

You can't get all the money this year; that's why they call it a career. Don Kyle

---

Lest this business look like a paved road to success, let me offer assurance that there was lots of struggling and starving as well. I was victim of the boom & bust cycle of market/deliver/starve/market/deliver that is so easy to fall into. I can remember when Chargex (now I'm dating myself!) introduced a new service allowing you to write a cheque against the credit card, and my waiting for the cheque book to show up in my mailbox so I could pay the rent.

While we enjoyed some success at bundling training programs into a broader system and showing managers how to take responsibility for sustainability, I also had the typical laundry list of topic offerings on the brochure. This was detrimental to standing out in the crowded market-place, as we weren't distinctive and perceived as specialists.

• My Best Success

NETWORKING AND CONNECTING EQUALS OPPORTUNITY

My biggest breakthrough and most valuable lessons came in the early 80s, when I was serving as a Canadian Rep on the Executive Council of the International Federation of T & D Organizations (where I met Ed Scannell and many others who are friends and colleagues today). You must get involved in the associations of your industry if you want to learn from the players who can help you broaden your perspective. I was invited to be honourary host at their international convention in Stockholm.

You decide when you stop speaking; they decide when the presentation is over. Warren Evans

---

Not a big job, but I got to introduce some keynote speakers. Two memorable ones were Mr. Jan Carlson, CEO of Scandinavian Airlines and Mr. Christian Gronroos, widely considered the father of The Nordic School of Service Management. Both of these visionaries spoke of a new approach to service. I had a chance to speak extensively with them, particularly Professor Gronroos, and was happy to find that their ideas were the same elements, which had been working in my approach.

I returned to Canada fired up and ready to focus my whole business on the area of service. While it seems obvious now, it was a serious gamble because no one was talking about "customer service" at the time, never mind service management. We incorporated The Service Excellence Group, and as an indication of how far ahead of the trend curve (or out on a limb) we were, I was also able to register the term'"Service Excellence" as a trademark in Canada.

We did massive amounts of research, and worked with clients to redesign our program offerings. By this time, the 'we' included Don Kyle, an OSA (Ontario Speakers Association) founder and long time professional speaker. We learned a great deal form each other, as we gained some implementation project contracts. We learned a great deal about what really worked and enjoyed some high-impact successes.

You can't luck into repeat business.
Anonymous

About six months later, Karl Albrecht's book, *Service America* was released. It seemed as that he'd picked up the same story a year earlier at a Amsterdam conference. Soon we were very busy, and the Group grew to eight consultants with various areas of expertise. Speaking quickly became my role, as I was asked to talk about what we were doing, and how we made it work, which fed the training and consulting business with new clients.

I also joined OSTD (Ontario Society for Training Development) in order to learn more about the industry and how to do business. There were nuggets of great value that helped me immensely. I learned that if you're going to be in a business, it makes sense to get involved with the associations that form its backbone, and that when you receive value from a valuable source, it's fair to also become a contributor by giving back to that organization.

• What I Would Do Over

SPECIALIZE AND GET INVOLVED SOONER

My great lesson was to focus real expertise in specific areas based on first-hand experience. We still did other things, but they weren't mentioned in our literature. Relationships were based on the expertise within our core topics, and then we would expand into other areas as needed. I wish I'd learned that sooner.

Another important lesson was to pass assignments outside our core topics to experts in those areas. While we passed up some immediate business, both our reputation and our profitability were enhanced. I wish I'd figured this out sooner as well.

By the mid 90's, I moved from away from consulting as a primary function to keynote speaking, and continued with some limited consulting. It was also time to move beyond the core topic of Service Management. A key piece of our "implementation process" had been the Strategic Retreat (for lack of a better succinct label). We'd done a number of these and always had great feedback.

An integral part of the retreats were the presentations on "horizon scanning / what's going on / where are the trends heading". I really enjoyed these and found them challenging, and also realized that over the last dozen years, we had built a track record for accuracy. It took about 3 years to make the transition to Future Trends.

One big marketing challenge that distinguishes this business is that most products don't have ego's. Warren Evans

---

Somewhere along the way the penny dropped for me that the old start-off line about'"more expertise looking at me than looking at you" was actually true. I stop taking myself so seriously and saw my role as less about telling them what they needed to know, and more about sharing my take on one piece of the trends puzzle; something they could add to their perspective and find it helpful in moving forward.

Few businesses provide the flexibility, fun and potential for good financial rewards as professional speaking, while offering opportunities to make significant contributions to the world around us. I 'm still traveling and learning.

CAPS

PROFESSIONAL TRAINERS,
FACILITATORS AND KEYNOTERS

Peggy Grall

Leadership Excellence, Managing Change, Conflict Resolution

Milton, ON Canada
Phone: 905-876-0149
Fax: 905-876-2235

PEGGY GRALL *is an internationally recognized Public Speaker, Executive Coach and Psychotherapist with 15 years experience in the areas of coaching, therapy, and leadership training. Her early career in managing business processes, combined with her work as a psychotherapist, and her understanding of leadership principles, has equipped her to provide effective guidance to leaders and teams. She presented over 600 workshops and presentations across the US and Canada, in the areas of: Achieving Leadership Excellence, Managing Change In the Workplace, Understanding and Enhancing Team Dynamics, Resolving Conflict, Capitalizing on Male & Female Work Styles, and Strategies For Personal & Professional Success.*

She is the past editor of Mental Health Matters—*a national magazine of the Mental Health Association and the current Editor in Chief of* Psychologica, *the trade magazine of The Association of Mental Health Professionals. She has been featured or quoted in a number of magazines and newspapers including:* The Human Resource Reporter, Halton Business Times, *as well as having her articles featured in:* Back On Track—*the Employment Canada newsletter,* Toronto Law Office Manager's Association *magazine and more.*

Peggy holds a Bachelor of Arts degree in Sociology & Anthropology, from the University of Guelph, and has completed Counseling Internship with the Toronto Institute Of Human Relations. She is currently completing Corporate Coach University's Certified Coaching program, which trains individuals from around the world in advanced corporate coaching skills.

• How I Got Started

My entrance into the speaking business was many years ago, on a sunny California afternoon. My husband was a seminary student in Oakland and I had been asked to speak to a group of women in San Francisco on the subject of "Sexuality and the Christian Woman." Well, I was all of 28 years old, married with 2 little children and couldn't imagine what I would know about sex that a group of women in San Francisco might want to hear! When I spoke to the conference organizer, I was told the group would likely be small and therefore appreciative of my efforts—not to worry.

There are lot's of people in your life who need to change, start with yourself. Peggy Grall

---

I practiced my talk with determination. I went over and over my lines, always in front of the mirror. I didn't want to look scared or embarrassed at the subject, even though, as the day approached, I became increasingly sure they had chosen the wrong woman for this job! What did I know about the finer points of sex, and theology? What did they want from me? The more I pondered the subject, the more I began to think the whole idea was a little odd. I comforted myself with a mental image of a few young women gathered to hear a couple of good ideas on bedroom technique.

The day came. I drove the 2 hours to the church where the conference was being held, accompanied by my pastor's wife and another friend. We walked into the large auditorium while the morning speaker was just finishing. Her subject was something about growing, learning and becoming. I could speak on that! That's easy, I thought. Why didn't they give me that subject? As I walked to the front row and took my place, I nervously fiddled with my papers and never really looked up until I was introduced. I never even looked at the person introducing me. I stiffly shot to the podium, arranged my papers and then looked up at the audience. There were hundreds of them! And they were all—every one of them—middle-aged, Afro-American women. I was stunned. I froze. I thought, "Oh no! I can't talk to them. I don't know what it's like to be their age, or a woman of color." And then my eye caught the gaze of one lovely, older woman in the front row. She was smiling broadly, nodding her head and softly saying, "Go on honey, we're listening." I swallowed hard, straightened myself and began.

At the end of every sentence I spoke, they said "amen". Every time I stopped to catch my breath, they called out, "you tell it sister", "I hear you", "that's right now". Each time I faltered, their chorus of voices would urge me on with, "Go on now".

If you want it perfect—don't do it live.
Unknown

I began to relax, to really see the words on the pages. I started to catch the momentum in the room. There was a rhythmic, dancing quality to their responses. I loved it! I said things that day about women and sexuality that I didn't even know I knew. I talked about personal dignity, privacy, joy and fulfillment. I spoke with pride, with humour, but mostly with such appreciation for these wonderful women's words of encouragement. They acted like everything I said was gold. They smiled, clapped and lifted me up as I spoke. They were the ultimate audience. They were a gift right from heaven, to the struggling new speaker that I was that day. I often thank the good Lord for putting me in front of them for my maiden voyage into the speaking profession. What a way to start!

• My Biggest Mistake

My biggest mistake—simply put, was not having the chutzpa to speak up for myself when I needed to. I had been asked by a third party to speak at a hospital on, "Getting Your Mind In Shape". I understood that topic to be, a standard Stress Management presentation. This presentation is usually light, upbeat, full of general information on exercise, positive thinking, etc. I never talked directly to the organizer and was going on the information I got from a friend of the organizer. Big mistake!

If you're not living on the edge, you're taking up too much room. African Proverb

---

When I arrived and was introduced to the woman introducing me, I casually asked her what kind of promotion they had done and, could I see it. When I looked at the flyer they had sent out, my teeth nearly dropped out of my head. They had described my talk as being, "a presentation on practical cognitive skills, mental exercises and techniques that professionals can use to keep their brains in shape". Oh no! That wasn't anything like the talk I'd brought! As the room filled up with doctors, nurses, and medical technicians, I foolishly decided that my only option was to try to make my presentation fit the description—and I had three minutes to do it in. I scrambled through the slides, frantically looking for anything and everything that even remotely fit the subject. When the introductions were done and I stood up, I just felt sick. I stumbled through the next 45 minutes, stammering, ad-libbing and generally doing both subjects a disservice. In hindsight I should have taken her aside, explained the oversight and then offered to proceed with my prepared presentation. I just lacked the confidence in myself to do that. I was still in the beginning stages of my speaking career and thought that the meeting planner was queen, and I was the lowly servant. Today, I'd handle that same scenario differently from the very beginning; no third party information, I'd see the promotional materials ahead of time, speak with the organizer personally and be fully informed about the audience and the expectations. Hindsight really is 20-20!

Our deepest fear is not that we are inadequate. Our deepest fear is that we are powerful beyond measure. It is our light, not our darkness, than most frightens us. We ask ourselves, Who am I to be brilliant, gorgeous, talented, fabulous? Actually, who are you not to be? Marianne Williamson

---

• My Best Success

My biggest success on the platform has come from becoming more focused on the audience and less on myself. I was hired as the keynote speaker at an annual conference in Philadelphia. This was to be my first big keynote and I was determined to be perfect! I shopped for weeks looking for just the right outfit, the right accessories and the perfect makeup for the occasion.

Throughout the entirety of my trip, Murphy's Law, "everything that can go wrong, will go wrong" prevailed. My flight was cancelled, the replacement flight was delayed, the airlines lost my luggage, and when I checked into the hotel, they had double booked my room! I was scheduled to be the kick-off speaker the next morning at 10:30. I got up early, spent 2 hours racing through the local mall buying something to wear, makeup and toiletries. I was rushed all morning, almost frantic as I stepped into the grand ballroom and up on the platform.

People will forget what you said. People will forget what you did, but people will never forget how you made them feel. Unknown

---

Due to the lack of time and my favorite products, my hair and makeup were, well—only passable. My outfit was too short, to tight and the wrong color. I didn't have time to buy shoes, so I was wearing 6-year-old penny loafers—with a suit! I have never considered myself to be overly vain, but that day I realized that I had focused a lot of my attention on myself as the speaker and not the audience. All the familiar trappings of personal security had been stripped away and I stood before them as—just me. I poured my heart and soul into that presentation. I smiled, I laughed, I sang (well, the whole group and I) and got my first standing ovation. I learned a valuable lesson that day. It's about them.

• What I Would Do Over

If I knew then what I know now, I'd have started this career earlier, been bolder and joined CAPS sooner. I love the speaking profession—I love it! It fits my lifestyle, my life purpose and my value system. It has taken me some time to realize that there are people who want to hear what I have to say. I guess, in the grand scheme of things, there is an audience somewhere for everyone. I'm finding mine. Speaking, as a profession offers travel, adventure, fun, flexibility, challenges, interesting people, good compensation, unique opportunities and the necessity to continually learn.

There are many things in life that will catch your eye, but only a few will catch your heart… pursue those. Unknown

---

What I wish I had done sooner is get better at marketing myself. Marketing is the part of the business (did I say business?) that I like the least. I started out thinking I could just avoid it. You know, maybe people would just call me up and want me to speak. I've learned the hard way that it doesn't work like that. You have to blow your own horn, tactfully of course, but nonetheless, blow it! I now have a web site, products for sale, marketing materials, etc. These have helped a great deal to get my name, and what I have to offer, out there. CAPS and NSA have been a very big part of my evolving business and speaking skill set. I happened onto CAPS almost accidentally; a friend suggested that, "if you're really going to do this, you should join a group". And what a group! I'm continually challenged, inspired and humbled, as I attend chapter meetings and conferences—rubbing shoulders with, and learning from, the best in the business.

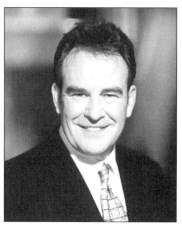

Bob Gray

The Backwards Memory Guy

Memory Edge Corporation

Whitby, ON Canada
Phone: 905-430-3115.
Fax: 905-430-5667.
E-mail: bobgray@memoryedge.com.
Web: **www.memoryedge.com**

BOB GRAY *provides tangible skills, which allow participants to work more efficiently, effectively and professionally through better recall, ultimately affecting the bottom line. He does this with unique humour and skills which have netted him a place in the* Guinness Book of World Records *as well as recent appearances on "Ripley's Believe It Or Not" and the NBC "Today Show".*

• How I Got Started

"You won't believe what this guy on my road crew can do. Bob, come up on stage!" It was a cold Saturday night at the "Studio in the Rockies" bar and saloon, Vail, Colorado in 1979 when I set foot on stage for the first time. Mike Mandel, a Canadian entertainer, whose gig was hypnotism, was the opening act for singer Tammy Wynette. I was, more or less, just along for the ride. A mutual friend had introduced me to Mike in Toronto the week before when out of the blue, he dropped the questions: "Do you like Tammy Wynette and would you like to go to Vail as part of my road crew?" I replied "No and Yes" respectively. A free trip to Vail seemed like a great idea.

Unfortunately, the job wasn't everything that it was cracked up to be. Aside from lifting and lugging a lot of heavy things, there was a long stretch of time when everyone quickly became bored. I tried to alleviate the gang's tedium with a few tricks I'd been practicing since I was a kid; my favourite was talking backwards, something I'd been able to do since I was 7 or 8 years old. By then I had driven my parents and my friends nuts with it, and I've always found it kind of fun to share it with new people. It seemed to work in Vail, and Mike in particular was left in hysterics every time I started babbling backwards.

The effectiveness of our memory banks is determined not by the total number of facts we take in, but the number we wish to reject. Jon Wynne-Tyson

---

On the last night of his weeklong gig, and without any warning, when Mike said those words into the microphone, I found myself on stage, suddenly sharing my odd quirk with a live audience. To my amazement, the audience applauded and I was hooked. For almost six years, Mike kept calling me up on stage to talk backwards. What started as simply reversing what was said to me graduated into a full act which incorporated my passion… memory.

———————

You are told a lot about your education, but some beautiful, sacred memory, preserved since childhood, is perhaps the best education of all. If a man carries many such memories into life with him, he is saved for the rest of his days. And even if only one good memory is left in our hearts, it may also be the instrument of our salvation one day.

Fyodor Dostoevski

———————

In September 1984, Mike and I went our separate ways and I entered the fitness industry. For the first time in my life I had a steady job (at least the pay cheques were steady) and I was determined to be the best I could. Although talking backwards didn't look too impressive on the resume, I knew a great memory wouldn't hurt. I adapted the memory systems I had been using since I was a child, and through them I was able to raise the retention rate of the club membership by 13 percent. My boss and colleagues were so impressed that I was asked to share the secret of my success at a national fitness convention, where once again, I found myself on stage. This time, I was primarily demonstrating my memory skills and teaching memory techniques, and only talking backwards as a bit of comic relief. Again, I was hooked. Now, presenting was even more fulfilling, knowing I was helping people become more efficient and effective through clear, simple and practical systems—those which had helped me through much of my life. Soon, the realization that what I had to teach could be applied to many other businesses and led me to making "speaking" a full-time career move.

• My Biggest Mistake

"Why did the chicken cross the road?" When I made the transition from entertainer to "speaker" I naturally wanted to keep some of the humour as an entertainment factor. However, for an entertainer, laughter exists pretty much for its own sake. There is no point to the punch line. I quickly learned that wit alone doesn't cut it when one presents to a group of business-minded people. Yes, they like to laugh and enjoy themselves just as much as anybody else. And, in fact, laughter has proven to be one of their most effective means of learning. But for both audience and presenter, laughter without relevance can be unfulfilling. The experience is like opening a birthday present and finding nothing inside. You have fun peeling off the fancy paper but ultimately you walk away disappointed.

So the answer is…"to get to the other side"…the learning and the laughter have to stick together.

The true art of memory is the art of attention.
Samuel Johnson

• My Best Success

Offering the budget conscious client an additional workshop the same day as my opening keynote. It shows a willingness to work with the client. I have one fee whether I speak for 45 minutes or a full day. Either way, my "inventory" is used. I love what I do and I love the opportunity to expand beyond my keynote. For me, it's as fulfilling as I hope it is for my students. And I call them students because by that time I believe they have gone beyond being a merely passive audience, and are now engaged with the process. Soon enough, these students will be using the systems in their workdays, becoming my best source of advertising.

• What I Would Do Over

My very first promotional video came about from a presentation that was large enough for me to be projected onto a giant screen for all to see. I asked if I could get a video copy of myself and I was told it wasn't actually being recorded. The camera was simply being used to project the image. The A/V guy suggested that if I wanted to pop a tape into the VCR back stage he would hit the record button and I would have a copy of the presentation. *Wow*, I thought. *What an inexpensive way of getting my first video*. The show went without a hitch, and the audience was even polite enough to laugh at all the right places, which made the recording even better.

The charm, one might say, the genius of memory,
is that it is choosy, chancy, and temperamental:
it rejects the edifying cathedral and indelibly
photographs the small boy outside,
chewing a hunk of melon in the dust.

Elizabeth Bowen

Here comes the mistake. For the sake of time, the tape needed a little editing. The people at the editing company managed to convince me that the tape could benefit from all sorts of wonderful computer graphics, slick editing techniques and music to make it even more impressive. Well, I was so blown away by what they could do that it blinded me to the actual quality of that original recording, especially the sound. It wasn't until I was fortunate enough to have another tape made, this one with good microphones, two cameras and two wonderful camera operators that I realized just how unprofessional the first video was.

So what I would have done differently would have been to save my money on fancy graphics and make sure the content was crisp, clean and crystal clear. Potential clients want to see you in action; they want to be able to hear what you have to say and they don't really care about fancy twirling special effects and nifty music. Special effects never leave a lasting effect. Make your message as bright as diamonds.

Angela Jackson

The Speaker With Heart

Angela Jackson Seminars

Phone: 416-259-3365
Web: **www.angelajackson.com**

ANGELA JACKSON, *known as "the speaker with heart," offers practical wisdom delivered with humor, compelling stories and audience interaction. Author of the best selling book* Celebrating Anger—Creative solutions for Managing Conflict at home, in relationships and on the job *and the soon to be published* Celebrating Life. *Angela has been featured on "Geraldo", "Real Life" and CBC "Venture's" television shows, as well as on radio and in print media.*

Challenging her audiences to think about what they need to know and do to create a future of optimism and success, Angela is committed to helping people grow not only in knowledge, but also in courage and confidence.

Her keynote presentations include: "Beyond your Wildest Dreams", "Success Strategies for the 21st Century", "Celebrating Anger" and "Living and Working with Heart." She also provides training in: Communication Skills, Conflict Management, Powerful Presentations and Transforming Stress.

A graduate of York University and University of Toronto, Angela thinks of herself as a forever learner. She lives with her husband and two cats, in Toronto.

• How I Got Started

I got into the speaking business by accident! Well, maybe it was more like going in through the back door. Let me tell you how it happened.

At that time, I was a high school Drama and English teacher, teaching kids who were having difficulty with the educational system. These were kids who'd recently arrived in Canada and couldn't speak much English. Or they were kids who were in trouble with the law, or they were living at a group home, or attending school sporadically because they were considered "slow". All these kids were lumped together in a secondary school and as you can imagine, many of them had behavioral issues.

One day my principal called me down to his office. Fearing the worst, I was taken aback when he asked me if I'd be interested in starting an anger workshop. Would I! I had just come from a classroom of thirty-two students who had anger issues and I was the angriest person in that room. Why was I so angry? Because my life wasn't working the way I wanted it to and I felt lonely and abandoned.

Do what you can, with what you have, where you are. Theodore Roosevelt

---

I was a single parent with two squabbling daughters and a younger accident-prone son. Most days I'd start off hollering at my kids to get up while I hastily dressed, rushed to put out their cereal, slapped together lunches and quickly downed my breakfast. Then I'd jump into my ancient rusty Buick, hoping it would make it safely to school and on time.

I taught about one hundred and eighty kids a day, and by the end of the day I was frazzled. Feeling like a punched-out boxer, I'd fall into the old Buick and head towards home, driving in a daze, thinking about my lackluster life. My kids didn't appreciate me; there was no money to get the car repaired, no time for rest and renewal, and I hadn't been on a date in years. I felt as if my life was a dead end street going nowhere.

Write it on your heart that every day is the best day of the year. Ralph Waldo Emerson

---

And then the principal's offer came! Fortunately he realized the importance of anger work and thought I'd make a good candidate!

I jumped at the opportunity. Although I had a background in psychology, I knew I needed more training, so I took every anger management course I could find, attending endless workshops, looking for the magic key that would open the anger lock. When it failed to materialize, I got inventive.

Sharing what you have is more important than what you have. Albert M. Wells, Jr.

By starting an anger lab after school, I began working with kids from my classes, kids who had attitude and resentments. After school we'd try out different techniques and create innovative role-plays and then the miracle began to happen. Kids who habitually punched others began to use words instead of fists. Kids who were depressed started to show a life spark. These were amazing results, which motivated me to keep on going, to use hands-on experiments and dig deep for solutions.

Word got around. Soon the parents began coming to my course, then the teachers and principals and after a couple of years I had a waiting list! I was so excited, so passionate about the work I was doing that I wanted to take it out to the world. I yearned to help people deal with negative patterns. To help others transform anger and fear into creative energy. And I wanted to do it full time.

Despite the fact that I had only a couple of hundred dollars in the bank, I left teaching and went for my passion. I made a red cardboard brochure, which I handed out at every networking event I could find. Nobody called. My first job came through a friend who paid me with a year's supply of batteries! My son thought this was wonderful, but it didn't put food on our table. I want you to know that hunger is a great motivator! I found an outdated copy of the MacLean-Hunter advertising guide and started calling companies on that list.

Nothing is impossible to a willing heart.
John Heywood

Prayer and persistence paid off, because one of those companies hired me. They sent me to Winnipeg to deal with their most taxing employees, which was right up my alley, after all, I'd been working with troublesome teens! I was on my way. "Conflict Management and Communication Skills" my three-day program, became a big success, netting me a two-year contract to present this program twice a month. I thought I was in heaven. I was doing work I loved, seeing people change in front of my eyes and getting well paid. Then one day, it was over. Every single employee in the Company had taken my course and I was out of work as quickly as I'd begun.

This taught me a valuable lesson. Don't put all the eggs in one basket (unless the basket has a life-long contract) and make sure you market while you work. (Sung to the tune of "Whistle while you work!")

After about five years of giving training programs I decided to try speaking. Why? Because it was the scariest thing I could imagine doing, other than sky diving, and I wanted to conquer my fear. So I set myself the goal of speaking. I thought that meant taking an hour from one of my training seminars and making it into a talk. Boy was I wrong!

This was in 1987. I'd given a few talks but had no knowledge of the speaking craft, for, as you are undoubtedly aware, speaking is a totally different arena from training.

And that's where CAPS came in and saved my career! A woman came up to me at the end of my stress management seminar and told me about CAPS, or OSA as it was then called. "The Ontario Speakers Association is a wonderful group of speakers who get together and share techniques and stories. You should check it out!" She gave me the OSA Board of Trade address, the Monday evening meeting schedule, and I have never looked back.

Joining CAPS was like being a solo swimmer who comes upon a miraculous hidden treasure. There they were: Alan Simmons, Vince Da Costa, Susan Duxter, Warren Evans, and Harold Taylor. Each week a new luminary, emitting a brilliant light, sharing their experiences, giving tips on what to do and how to do it.

_____

When you have learned to love, you have learned to live. Angela Jackson

_____

I sat in the audience mesmerized, thinking I could never do what they were doing. It seemed so effortless, so flawless, and yet, at the same time I was inspired to use the techniques that were being offered, motivated to develop my own style and stories. It was exciting, intimidating and for me, revolutionary. I had not imagined such a world existed. I'd been like a goldfish swimming outside the goldfish bowl who suddenly sees other fish with similar fins and swims home. For CAPS was my home then and still is today, some fifteen years later.

We've changed in the meantime. We've grown bigger, with chapters now in most major cities. When we get together for our annual conference, we number three hundred instead of thirty, but that same friendly spirit, that welcoming hometown warmth is still there and we keep extending our hands and hearts to others, sharing our experiences and knowledge.

Good company in a journey makes the way seem shorter. Izaak Walton

---

We're the only organization I know that teaches our competitors all of our tricks! We even pay to do this! We pay full admission to speak at our conferences, because that's the model we got from our "parent," the National Speaker's Association. Giving back what we've received is how we grow. We're a generous, committed group of speakers and trainers who care about each other, and that's our strength and our success.

• What I Would Do Over

If I had to do it all again, I would join CAPS the moment I even thought about training or speaking. I would rush to the nearest chapter and soak up the information and inspiration. I'd learn techniques and immediately get active in my chapter, because that is how we became part of our association. I'd throw myself totally into this business and give it all I had, because through giving we expand and become something more, something that truly touches hearts and transforms lives.

Kelly McCormick

THᴇ MᶜCORMICK TᴇAM INC.

Toronto, ON Canada
Phone: 416-690-8275
E-mail: kelly@mccormickteam.com
Web: **www.mccormickteam.com**

KELLY McCORMICK *gets people's attention. She likes to think it's her outstanding sense of style, but they tell her it's because the punch line comes first, the laugh second, and then they realize the "ah-ha" moments were there all along.*

This Second City Improv alumni's approach to **"Enhancing Effectiveness When Working With Others"** *really works.*

> *"…tremendous performance…your understanding of our leaders and the challenges came through loud and clear"*
>
> American Society of Interior Designers.

> *"(Kelly) obviously has a great deal of experience in the 'real' world…"*
>
> Supervisor, City of Toronto

Fueled and inspired is how participants leave the sessions, whether it's a keynote for a large group or a small workshop.

Great audiences from numerous countries, come from private and public sectors, colleges, associations, foundations, municipalities, government, consultants and businesses.

• **How I Got Started**

The line at the local bakery was long. Finally, it was my turn. In a confident voice I placed my usual order. "Three cheese buns and a cinnamon roll." Nothing out of the ordinary. Except on this particular night something was different. Something had caught the attention of the dark haired man standing next to me. Something so compelling in my delivery that he had taken notice.

Maybe it was the perfect pitch. Perhaps it was the intentional pause after the word 'three' and before the word "cheese" that caused him to turn his head and lock eyes with me. What really mattered was he had heard me. The next thing I knew the stranger was pulling a neatly typed contract, on forty pound high quality paper, out of the bag clasped under his arm. A golden tipped pen was thrust in my hand and that was it. I was a professional speaker.

It's been a dizzying action packed ride. The last ten years have been filled with standing room only auditoriums, cheering crowds and the continuous strobe of camera flashes. There are plans for my own syndicated talk show morning and afternoon, a six-deal book tour and a big hair makeover!

Okay, okay, so a little creative license was taken in re-writing my history.

Miss Frost, the smartest kindergarten teacher in the whole world actually foresaw my destiny. "Kelly is a very influential little girl... she spends a lot of time chatting with others."

Looking back, paramount in my life has always been speaking, entertaining and exchanging information, even when chatting with others. It's only the venues that have changed over the years.

Get out of your house. Get out of your head.

Kelly McCormick

Transitioning from being a talker in Miss Frost's class to becoming a professional speaker can be attributed to many key things. An important discovery was understanding the difference between how and where opportunities would appear.

Today a statement I share with audiences is "get out of your house, get out of your head." So how did I get into this business? By getting out of the house and out of my head.

The game plan was to intentionally talk to people. Internal dialogue, including unanswered questions about the industry, the best fit, how to get started and how to keep going, became the external dialogue.

Necessity is the mother of invention. We've all heard it. I lived it. The determination to get my business off the ground contributed to the development of the three part question, "do you know, do you know someone who knows, or do you know where I could find out?"

Inevitably someone would provide the exact information needed just when it was required. Even casual comments given in passing enabled the next step to be taken. Many times, the next step came to me from a direction I hadn't even looked.

During this process another powerful and surprising outcome was surfacing. A community of mutual support was being built.

• My Biggest Mistake

It was year one of my speaking career. The blue suit was a good choice. It was eight p.m. and I was standing center stage at the "Women in Business and Recreation" meeting.

Everything was in place. A stellar blurb had been written for the promo material. The benefits had been outlined and the title was catchy, "Powerful Communication for Powerful Business Connections".

The house lights dimmed. The Association President cleared her throat. She began to deliver a heart-felt introduction, "Tonight, we are very fortunate to have Kelly McCormick from The McCormick Team speaking to us (drum roll please) on Networking to Meet a Life Partner."

What! What did she just say? What do these people think I'm speaking about? Note to self, my career is over!

Lessons were learned. Always request to see any changes to copy, before materials go to print. Also, ask that final promotional materials be sent to you. For some unknown reason there are editing fairies at the printers who can also change the changes you've just approved.

Risking is moving past your acceptable limits.
Author Unknown

Do you wonder what happened at the women's association talk? After silently calming my rapid breathing, I gazed across the room, slowly smiled and began to speak. "As this is an association for business and recreation we have a terrific opportunity to turn powerful business communication into powerful life-partner communication. After all, finding one's life partner can sometimes seem like a career!"

• My Best Success

Some of the success has come from not speaking, a real oxymoron for a professional speaker. The art of observing the audience's subtle, non-verbal communication has indicated the internalization of points made, confirmed that issues close to the heart have been addressed, expressed shared experiences, and enabled me to lead the audience where they needed to go.

It's not always about the speaker.
It's about the audience. MG

• What I Would Do Over

If I knew then that there was a tremendous opportunity to impact positive change in peoples' lives, I would have moved from talking to professional speaking a whole lot sooner.

———————————————

Just go for it kid. Bob (Dad) McCormick

———————————————

Maggie Milne

Oh!riginality

Phone: 800-587-1767
Fax: 807-939-3001
E-mail: maggie@tbaytel..net
Web: **www.originalmaggie.com**

MAGGIE MILNE *is the Oh!riginality Specialist, Keynote Speaker, and Master of Ceremonies.*

Her firm, MMI (1986) has a reputation for zealous, highly inter-active programmes with a twist of ingenuity. Maggie simplifies Strategic Systems Thinking theory to stretch minds and funny bones with creative stories about people and their organizations, whether she is presenting in a mudhut in Ghana or a boardroom in Australia or Canada.

Maggie is a founding member of the Board of Directors of CAPS, the Canadian Association of Professional Speakers, currently acting as National Director of Membership. She belongs to the International Coach Federation and the World Clown Association, as "Magnolia."

In 2001, Maggie was the inaugural recipient of the Northern Ontario Business Influential Women's Alumni Award for "demon-strating phenomenal influence as an inspiration to others."

• How I Got Started

HALF NAKED ON A CROOKED PEW

Call this the profession of the obedient rebel. Learn the rules. Know the game but simultaneously change it, mold it, surprise yourself in the most mundane of moments. Climb up, step off the precipice of each challenge. Glide through the story, punctuate the point, land half naked in full view of the audience. And never get too comfortable sitting on the crooked pew.

Some things turn me on, as if I'd swallowed a neon sign. Smoke Blanchard, high-altitude climber

---

Who me, a speaker? It took thirty six years to figure out that my latent rebellious nature was the perfect match with an audience.

No matter how hard I tried, I could not blend in with the acceptable career path for girls in the seventies. I was successful despite myself, whether my contract of the moment left me in the tangles of bureaucracy or the rat-infested bowels of northern grain elevators. That twist of curiosity buried in my bones repeatedly led me from the mundane pay cheque to the exploration of wild and wonderful turf. Security was never my middle name. Until this...

My Mentor believed that I could make it solo. Now, after sixteen years in the speaking biz, I am content to sit half naked on a crooked pew. My clients have taught me that baring my idiosyncrasies creates a powerful Velcro stickiness between the speaker and her audience. I have discovered the spirit and soul attached to every learning point. Time after time, I have taken the challenge of the crooked path, to look for the odd way around the apparent simplicity. I have learned to sit on that pew, to contemplate and pause instead of continually looking for the maverick's version of life. Not fitting in has led to fitting in.

I have come to love the fiery tenderness of the platform; just let me do it one more time!

• My Biggest Mistake

CREEPY CRAWLY UNDIES

I can handle almost anything that the crowd throws at me. Literally. Like comments of the eloquent expert. Or the babbling saboteur. Even the total bomb of my material with the demanding Meeting Planners Convention. It's all a piece of cake, compared to my very first speech.

Miss Plunkett, the Ogre, demanded perfection in her Grade 6 classroom. She assigned the topic "Canadian Pioneers" with expectations of solid research and prolific delivery. I wanted an A+, so grandma became my accomplice in the project, designing an authentic pioneer costume complete with flour-sack apron. I became Katherine Hepburn, thriving in hardship. {Look skyward. Wipe sweat off brow!} It was the perfect performance, until my training bra snapped. I lost it.

Astound me. Try your hardest. These last flashes of astonishment are what I cannot live without.

Colette, Earthly Paradise

Thirty years later, it happened again. Not once, not twice… underwear has become my Achilles heal.

In fact, my first appearance with a CAPS audience was the re-enactment of that pre-teen moment without the drama. I was nervous. I dressed carefully; *Ta-dah! Here we go*, I thought. Five minutes later, my pantyhose disintegrated.

My lower half took on the motionless stance of a nun in prayer. I could have bet my puppy that the folks in the front row could hear the downward swoosh of the panty-part of the hose, as it slid down my hips and took its place just above my hemline, close to my knees. I waddled through that presentation with poise, smiled with grace, and sunk back into Miss Plunkett's C+ grade zone. Underwear had done me in. Again.

I have since invented the female version of a body-length jock strap which is glued in strategic places. Gravity may have pulled some body parts down, but I'll be danged if my underwear ever escapes again!

• My Best Success

SURPRISE! MASTER OF CEREMONIES

A colleague pulled me aside after my stint as Master of Ceremonies at the CAPS convention. He said, "Maggie, how do you DO that? You are the best M.C. I have seen; in fact, you are northern Ontario's version of Whoopi Goldberg!".

Now that was a compliment and a half! I asked him to put it in writing. Yet the seriousness of the comment was lost to me until I really started thinking about "how" I emcee. What did I do that others were not doing?

As I watched other volunteer M.C.'s behind the lectern that day, I scribbled on the back of the conference brochure:

- The role of Master of Ceremonies can build business for you, expose your talents to new audiences in unexpected ways, or destroy your reputation. People may assume that because you speak proficiently, you are also a master M.C.

- Leap of faith! Not necessarily so!

I gasped when colleagues mispronounced names, stumbled through directions to the party busses waiting outside the hotel, and scrambled for folded hunks of notes. Some took the opportunity to present a mini-keynote, stealing time from the presenter waiting behind the curtain. "They don't get it!" I said to myself.

It was an "Aha!" moment for me. Speaking and M.C.'ing demand different skill sets.

The role of M.C. requires you to step back from the limelight and become the creative glue for the event. You are the director of a seamless production, the timing fanatic and the magician who turns mundane announcements into memorable short pieces. You are the glitch patcher, the curiosity "piquer", the one who sets the scene. You are central control. You are the welcome smile, the bridge between segments and the dot-to-dot connector. You are in charge, but in the background.

That poignant comment from a CAPS member, led me to formalize my Master of Ceremonies line of business. He inspired me to unearth a latent talent, to change. From the Master podium, "Thanks!"

Nature loves to hide. It rests by changing.
Heraclitus

• What I Would Do Over

LOOK CLOSER TO HOME

A wise person once said that what is most obvious is most invisible. The answers are hidden in our pockets, under our noses, and in our hearts. This is what I have learned:

1. My entrepreneurial parents were very smart business partners. As a photographer, my dad "Dan's formula for Customer Service," was deceptively simple. "Do whatever it takes over and over again. Do it better, over and over again. Do it smarter. Faster." My parents' accents sounded as heavy as strawberry syrup on creamy rice pudding, yet they communicated excel-

lence with every breath. Thirty years later he still receives compliments from customers. Could I do this too?

2. My grandmother was the epitome of loving kindness, layered with an expectation for discipline. In this age of raw crisis, stress and war, it is important to crawl into the safety and warmth of grandma-like acceptance. Her memories remind me of the touch and smell of flannelette. How can I bring more flannelette—or polar fleece—into my life and the hearts of our audiences?

3. My Mentor and I would take "voltas", Greek for long, meandering walks. We would chat about political correctness, cutting through red tape, what it takes to just get along around here. He would ask me questions which seemed unrelated to the discussion at hand. He would dig deep, but gently discard layer upon layer of old skin. As a mentor myself, am I as adept at questioning, steering and gently guiding? Who is mentoring whom as we stroll down the path?

If I had to do it over again, I would not hesitate since because the best answers may just be hidden in that tortilla between gigs.

Everybody loves something, even if it's only tortillas. T. Rinpoche

---

Productivity Morale Wellness

Rosalie Moscoe, RNCP

Toronto, ON Canada
Phone: 416-636-1560
Toll Free: 800-506-4333
E-mail: rosalie@healthinharmony.com
Web: **www.healthinharmony.com**

ROSALIE MOSCOE's mission is to provide corporations and associations with the tools for their people to deliver more value through increased productivity, boosted morale and wellness. Through her keynote addresses or seminars, Rosalie creates an inspirational and exhilarating learning atmosphere, helping people to adapt to our changing world.

Rosalie is a Wellness Consultant, having graduated from Centennial College's postgraduate, Wellness & Lifestyle Management Program in 1995. She is a Registered Nutritional Consultant Practitioner, a graduate of the Canadian School of Natural Nutrition 1998, and is in private practice. In 1999, she taught "A Wellness Approach to Stress Management" at Centennial College.

Prior to her speaking career, Rosalie was a children's singer and performer, having recorded five children's albums and was nominated for two Juno awards. Through empathy, humour, caring and mutual respect, she brings her wit, energy, passion (and sometimes song) to the speaking platform.

• How I Got Started

Some people feel that speaking in front of an audience is a fate worse than death. For me, the adrenaline flows and gives me an opportunity to be "on"—teaching, sometimes singing, using humour—hopefully inspiring others towards their self-development. My career started when I was three years old when I upstaged my six-year-old brother at his holiday concert. He was scheduled to sing a song, but I too knew every word of that song, having practiced at home with him. Although I had never before been in front of an audience, I instinctively raced backstage, and when the curtain rose, two children instead of one began to sing.

Throughout my teen years and twenties, I delved into the arts, singing, dancing and playing musical instruments. When I married and became a young mother, I sang at my children's nursery school, and was later employed by various pre-schools and libraries to give music classes for youngsters.

Success must be a shared experience.

Mary Kay Ash

I embarked on a professional career as a children's singer and performer as part of the Canadian singing duo "Jim & Rosalie," which lead to a solo career for a few years. I recorded five albums, published a music and activity book and was nominated for two Juno awards in 1981 and 1982. Like many women with a family, I was taking on too much. My health was being affected. I looked for ways to reduce stress, studied relaxation techniques and changed my diet. My health steadily improved.

I became so interested in the whole area of preventive health that I returned to college to study Wellness & Lifestyle Management and later, Nutrition. The inspiration to share this knowledge with others launched my speaking career. It was fun to be on stage again, for in my heart, I was still a performer. Only this time, people in the audience were somewhat taller (yet still liked to have fun)! Being a member of CAPS helped me gain professionalism in a brand new career.

I found that audiences appreciated my singing—especially "I'm All Stressed Out" to the tune of "I'm All Shook Up" when I delivered my "Less Stress: More Success!" program. The *Singing Speaker* soon became my trademark. Other clients asked me to include songs such as "Butterfly, Flutterby" a song about self growth when I presented "Extreme Self-Care for Women" or "I love my Chocolate" a song that I sing at the beginning of my "Power Foods for Productivity" seminar.

You never achieve real success unless you like what you are doing. Dale Carnegie

---

Presently, I work either as a speaker on the platform presenting various wellness-related topics or as a nutritionist, providing one-to-one counselling for the patients of two medical doctors. Whether it's in my private practice, or on stage imparting positive messages, it brings me joy and fulfillment to touch people's hearts, to help them move forward as their lives (and mine) unfold.

• My Biggest Mistake

My biggest mistake on the platform was being an amateur in a professional setting. In my early years, I was asked to do a seminar for a Fortune 500 company. I was fairly new in the business and felt this job was a little over my head, but I took it anyway and behaved like the rookie I was. I used an overhead projector—not cool with this large company. I taped "Words of Wisdom" to their walls, on laminated posters. It was a hot day and the posters systematically peeled themselves to the floor as I was speaking. Without an in-depth knowledge of the audience, I couldn't properly relate to them. I was pretty devastated by the evaluations, but it was an outstanding learning experience.

Success… is connecting with the audience.

Rosalie Moscoe

Now I conduct myself as a professional. I use an interesting, attractive Power Point™ presentation and have overheads as a backup. I interview a few people who will be in the audience and either meet with the organizers or send out a questionnaire to obtain as much information about the company as possible. I find out what their problems are and what challenges they face. All this information helps me better understand my audience, for then and only then, can I deliver real value. Success in the speaking business is about connecting with the audience and having a burning desire to give them a dynamic and unique experience that can make a dramatic difference in their lives.

• My Best Success

My biggest success came from taking an active interest in life-long learning—especially about the speaking business. At a NSA convention I attended a few years ago, fate had me sit beside a speaking coach, Burt Dubin (www.dubinspeak.com). Investing in his course and working with him was the start of my success in the speaking business. He not only coaches me as to what to do with regards to marketing, promotion, speaking techniques and writing articles, but also provides me with materials on every aspect of the speaking business.

One very important exercise was to investigate "the spirit of the speaker." I needed to find out why I was speaking and what I wanted to impart to my audiences. I needed to be more passionate about my topics, more confident about what I had to say. I learned to incorporate more of who I am as a person—one who likes to have fun and feels compassion toward people. I also learned that it was important to become very knowledgeable in my topics—to become "an expert who speaks." The more I learn about my topics, the more confident I feel on the platform. In this information age of rapid change, we need to read, research, listen to people and interview others.

• What I Would Do Over

If I had to do it all over again knowing then what I now know I would have become more organized and more inquiring about technology earlier in my career. My office and filing system were disasters. Sometimes I was avalanched under mounds of paper. I could never find anything. A few years into my speaking career, I was asked to deliver a Time Management seminar and when I researched the topic, I realized how disorganized I was! I was missing appointments and felt like a scatterbrain. In those early years, I could barely operate my computer and wasn't particularly interested in learning more about it. I started to change some old habits that weren't working anymore.

Education will never become as expensive as ignorance. Unknown

---

Now, my office and computer files are in order and I feel more in control. I'm organized and resist the temptation to collect clutter. My day-timer is my bible, but I try to remain open and flexible at the same time. I get administration help when I need it and have learned a lot more about the computer, through courses and one-to-one learning. If I had been more open to new technology at the beginning of my career, I would have saved a lot of time, energy and money.

I see that technology is taking us by storm and as speakers, we need to be ready. I recently delivered my first audio teleconference. Anything new is a bit scary. I did my research and learned a lot from just giving the talk. I remembered Reva Nelson's words: "Sometimes we have to *risk it*". My next new venture is an E Learning seminar. It's exciting to be at the edge of new ground breaking technology. It's new for all of us, but it's the way of the future. Just "go for it!"

Sometimes we have to risk it.

Reva Nelson

Humor, Magic & Energy

Mississauga, ON Canada
Phone: 888-407-9995
Fax: 905-281-9959
E-mail: sunjay@sunjaynath.com
Web: **www.sunjaynath.com**

Sunjay Nath, MBA, BSc Eng

SUNJAY NATH *is a graduate of Queen's University Engineering and has a Wilfrid Laurier University MBA. Sunjay has been speaking professionally for over seven years. His travels have taken him across Canada and the U.S.*

His ability to relate to people comes from his many experiences. Sunjay is a Black belt in Taek Won Do, the recipient of major awards in business and youth achievement, and an amateur magician. He is also a former camp director and director of an e-Learning company. Humour, magic, energy and integrity are the keys to his success with audiences of all ages.

• How I Got Started

CAMPAIGNS

In high school, I was very involved with academics and extra-curricular activities. This gave me the opportunity to attend many conferences, workshops and other functions. In particular, I remember a leadership conference I attended as a grade 10 student. The conference was very motivating and inspiring. Organizers brought in wonderful speakers to address the group on achieving our potential and living up to our dreams. As I sat in the audience as a 15 year-old in awe, I thought to myself, "Someday I would like to come back and inspire future participants of this program just as these speakers have inspired me!" I didn't think too much about it other than that and I didn't even know that speaking could be a profession.

I am a great believer in luck, and I find the harder I work, the more I have of it. Stephen Leacock

---

While I was completing high school, I kept attending various leadership gatherings, again seeing great speakers in action. Beginning with that first conference, I stayed involved in many different capacities as a gofer, a counselor and as an executive alumni member. By graduation, I was living much of what had been taught to me by speakers (GIGO = good stuff in, good stuff out)—I was student council president, valedictorian, active in theatre and sports, ran the school store, and carried an average in the high 90s. After high school, I went off to study engineering at Queen's University. I wasn't totally committed to the idea of being an engineer, but everyone told me that with my strong math and science background it would be best.

During my second year at university, I got the call! The president of student council at my old high school asked me to give a pep talk to my old high school about the advantages of getting involved within the school. "We'll pay you to speak," she said. Flashes of having the same impact as previous speakers had had on my life went through my head and I started to really get excited. My roommate caught a glimpse of my excitement and inquired why I was so happy.

I never did a day's work in my life— it was all fun. Thomas Alva Edison

---

After I explained, she offered a great opportunity for rehearsal. "I coach a swim team," she said. Why don't you come and practice on us?" Within a couple of days, I met the head coach and we talked about a potential program for the swimmers. The next thing I realized, I was waking up at 6:00 a.m. Saturday mornings to talk to 8-10 year-olds about setting goals, going after their dreams, communicating effectively with their parents and how all this applied to swimming. That was both challenging and extremely rewarding—you should see the thank-you notes I received, handwritten in crayon.

• My Biggest Mistake

MIGRAINES

The biggest mistake I have made—and the sad truth is I have made it often, is I forget to be me on the platform. As silly as that sounds, my largest failures on stage have come when I tried to give the audience what I think they want, even if I have to pretend I am someone else to do so.

Years ago, I was asked to do some work with a business networking group. Generally, I am told my presentations are fun and high energy—couple this with the fact that I looked very young and I started to second-guess my delivery style. What if I went up in front of the group and did "my thing" but no one in this highly conservative group took me seriously. So, to avoid embarrassment, I totally changed my style. I was very serious, I was very professional, I was very conservative, I was very much not myself, I was trying to be someone else … and worst of all—I very much stunk. There is nothing wrong with this style of delivery, but it is not for me and the audience clearly saw that.

More recently, I was asked to address 250 bank managers from Scotiabank. Again, the same fears went through my head. This time, the last thought in my head was "I am going up there and I will do 'my thing.' If they don't like it, I will find an audience that does." The result was a standing ovation from the highly conservative group and a call three weeks later from Scotiabank for another opportunity to speak.

The tongue is the only tool that gets sharper with use. Anonymous

---

Currently I am prepping a session that I am delivering next month in Ohio where I will address 6000 participants—I am very excited and the *butterflies taste great*! Regardless of how the presentation goes, I can promise that when I am on stage I will be me! My biggest mistake is when I forget that.

• My Best Success

GAINS

That session with the swimmers lasted 8 weeks, and with each week, the crowd grew larger and larger. At first, some of the older swimmers sat in on the sessions, then the parents. By week four, instead of having the twelve 8-10 year-old swimmers, I had about 40 people ranging in age from 4 (younger brothers and sisters) to 60 (grandparents), plus parents and of course, the swimmers.

A gentleman approached me after one session and offered me a "gig" speaking to a youth group. I gratefully accepted. After all, I was having a blast with the Kingston Blue Marlins Swim Team. At the conclusion of the youth group talk, I was handed an envelope—to my surprise there was money in it. I refused it. "I am doing this for fun," I insisted.

————————

There is nothing wrong with having nothing to say, unless you insist on saying it. Anonymous

————————

The response was, "We're just sorry we couldn't give you more. What you have given us is worth it." Even better, once again an audience member who thought I would be just the right person to speak at another venue approached me. She wanted to know how much I charged. She was a teacher at a local high school, and she wanted *me* to speak! At that point I realized that I was on to something; I started reading the books, listening to the tapes and asking questions to anyone and everyone that could help. I was entering the field of professional speaking.

Since the swim team, I have addressed 300,000 participants in keynote presentations, workshops and facilitation sessions across Canada and in the US. I have addressed audience members that range in age from 4 years old to 80 years old, from CEOs of companies to CEOs of sandboxes—and I have absolutely loved it! People ask why I didn't pursue a career in engineering. Well, I like engineering, but I *love* speaking—and there is a world of difference between the two. And, for the past 7 years, I have spoken to the delegates of that first leadership conference I attended as a grade 10 student.

• What I Would Do Over

INGRAINS

Although some have said I have come a long way, there remains a long journey ahead of me. I still actively read books, listen to tapes, ask the questions and I still get butterflies. Each presentation is a new group, a new talk or a new time and things will not always go as planned—but there are sooo many opportunities.

What would I do now? As a speaker, if I don't have passion, I will stop speaking. There is nothing worse than not believing your own message. The minute I am no longer excited and eager to speak is the minute I will stop speaking. If I were just starting today I would be passionate in my choice of topics. There is no substitute for passion. If you are motivated about your topic, it will show and it will make you successful.

Character is determined by what you accomplish when the excitement is gone. Anonymous

---

When I first started speaking, the best bit of advice that was shared with me was, "Sunjay, if you want to be an effective speaker, you need two things. First, have story to tell. Second, have a burning desire to tell it." That advice still applies today, Have those two elements and everything else will fall into place. With that in mind, I have found that what they say is true—when you find something you love to do, you'll never have to work!

Reva Nelson

Inspirational words lead to positive actions

Words.Worth
Keynotes & Seminars

Phone: 416-656-0994
E-mail: revan@istar.ca
Web: **www.revanelson.com**

REVA NELSON, *President of Words.Worth since 1985, is known for her informative workshops, honest facilitation and inspiring keynotes that shift people toward clarity and action. Reva has a background in psychology, education, theatre and business and is the successful author of* Risk It! *and* Bounce Back! *Her powerful presentations re-energize clients in finance, insurance, pharmaceuticals, health, education, government and many associations world wide. With refreshing, down-to-earth information, straight forward consulting and entertaining keynotes, Reva Nelson helps clients meet the challenges of personal and corporate change.*

> *"Your keynote dealing with risk-taking and change was very targeted and established the proper framework for our off-site."*
>
> *CEO, Global Securities*

KEYNOTE TOPICS:

- Bold Brave Chickens!—Positive Risk-taking
- From Bleak to Peak!—Resilience
- Guts Gusto!—Intuition at work

- Common Sense Isn't Common Enough!

CONFERENCE AND WORKSHOP TOPICS:

- Positive Risk-taking for Powerful Results
- Bounce Back! Creating Resilience from Adversity
- Can We Talk? Improving Communications
- Speak Easy—Panic-Free Presentation Skills
- Living Leadership and Values
- Do You Want Fries With That? Getting More Business

(Copyright titles and concepts, Reva Nelson, 2002)

FACILITATION:

Reva Nelson was a facilitator for CIBC's residential 6-day leadership program for over four years. She often stays with a company after her keynote to facilitate their next initiatives.

For more information on Reva Nelson's positive and powerful approach, or to order books, call 416-656-0994, e-mail revan@istar.ca or visit www.revanelson.com

• How I Got Started

I was a brand new, first year teacher. It was a cold, brilliantly sunny February afternoon in London, Ontario. My grade 2 class was working hard on their individual projects, surprisingly with a longer than usual attention span. Out of the blue, 7 year old Dulcie came up to my big oak desk, full of attitude and vigor. "MS. Nelson," she says, emphasizing the Ms. because it was a new term for them. "I was just wondering something."

"Yes, Dulcie, what is it?" I answered, smiling at this spunky kid who I just adored.

"I was wondering, what would you be doing if you weren't here teaching us?"

I was so taken aback by the question, I replied spontaneously and intuitively.

Out of my mouth popped, "I think I'd like to try acting."

Dulcie fixed her huge brown eyes on mine and said, "Well, you'd better go do it then, doncha think?"

I felt as if lightning had struck. I had no idea why I said acting. I was basically shy, except with kids, and had last acted in grade one. I had no experience, no knowledge of how to start. But start I did. I quit teaching, to the surprise and dismay of my parents, my principal and my friends. I "lucked" into a summer theatre project, a part-time teaching job and eventual acting jobs in London and Toronto. I acted for 5 years, earning my professional ACTRA and Equity designations.

Life is a dance partner waiting for us to take the first step; then lead with passion and joy.

Reva Nelson

Peter Senge says, "It's not what vision is, it's what vision does."

I didn't get on the Johnny Carson show, I wasn't a Broadway star, but I acted and I loved it. Later, I taught again, moved onto counselling in student services at a University, co-ordinated conferences, saw seminar leaders and thought "Aha! That's what I want to do." I started developing workshops and eventually keynotes. My client list grew from government to international corporations.

To know, trust and act from your own truth is the most essential risk of all. Reva Nelson

---

The ability to trust my creativity to improve businesses and lives came from one little girl who challenged me to move forward in ways that neither she, nor I, could ever have imagined.

• My Biggest Mistake

Thomas Edison, who knew a few things about creativity, said that he had no failures, only attempts that taught him something. In this light, pun intended, I will share some of my attempts that taught me something!

1. OFFICE MANAGEMENT:

I really fall down in the "stay in touch" category. If people want me they pretty much have to find me! The NSA comment is, "There's a million dollars in your filing cabinet." The fix? I need to use the equipment and systems I already have!

2. MARKETING:

I have been in the business so long (since 1985 in Toronto) that I can do workshops and seminars and training and coaching and facilitating and keynoting—only not everyone knows that! I'm only now learning to "drive the business". I had great success with *Risk It!*, my first book, by doing a lot of media interviews. With *Bounce Back!* I was just too busy to market it properly. It still made money, but not as much as it could.

3. OOPS!:

a) Years ago, before laptops, I was doing four different seminars for the same client, many times over several months. It was inevitable… I turned up with all the materials and overheads for "Meetings for Results" when the topic was "Panic-free Presentation Skills." I didn't panic, but that's why I always ask for a flip chart and markers to be in the room.

b) I accepted an after dinner keynote with a group that turned out to be quite drunk and really needed a comic or a D.J. ...not me. I kept on as best I could, but when I talked with the meeting planner the next day and suggested they don't get a speaker in that time slot again, she replied, "Do you know, my last five speakers all had that same suggestion?"

c) Of course I once tripped and fell onto the cutest guy in the room. It happens.

• My Best Success

There are two really, one from trusting my intuition on a topic and the other from being a "nice guy."

There is no grief which time does not lessen or soften. Cicero

---

1. It was years ago, when women's networking groups were just beginning to form. I spoke on trusting your gut to take career risks; afterward, many women were asking me how to take risks. I put a program together, even though I thought I was quite a chicken myself, but they loved it. Then I asked the Director at the Human Resources Secretariat, where I was already giving presentation and meeting skills seminars if he thought risk was an important topic for both men and women. He got all excited, pulled out the executive profile sheet and said, "We've only had Outward Bound programs to address this skill of risk-taking. You put it together and I'll pay you to present it here as one of our workshops." No one else thought Positive Risk-taking" was a viable idea, or if they did, they were suggest-

ing I call it leadership or empowerment—anything but what it really was. I tied it into creativity and innovation and ran it there for four years—thanks to one Director who believed in the idea and me.

The ultimate lesson which all of us have to learn is unconditional love, which includes not only others but ourselves as well. Elisabeth Kübler-Ross

---

2. The second instance was tied into "Risk-taking" as well. As a special favour to a very good friend, I agreed to present at her friend's event, the gay businessman's network gala valentine's evening. June Callwood, who I admired greatly, was the other speaker. They asked me to stretch my topic to become, "The Risks of Falling in Love" to suit the gala. I decided to have fun with it, joked around a lot, felt like the Bette Midler of the speaking world, but also made the point that I'm usually speaking about business risk-taking to corporate audiences. Someone told someone, who told someone, and he called to ask where my book "Risk It!" was available. We got to chatting, and he said he was a consultant on leadership. I said, "Well, I've never heard of you." He replied, laughing, "Well I never heard of you either." We became fast friends, and then he suggested I contact CIBC's leadership centre immediately as they needed just one more facilitator. That call became an interview which led to a 5 year contract of the most wonderful work on leadership, mind sets, values and team development with some of the top facilitators in Ontario. It was lucrative, educational, fun and rewarding—all from a most unusual keynote speech, given as a favour to a friend.

• What I Would Do Over

It's been a long ride over 17 years. It's been a journey with bumps, scrapes, bruised egos and missed opportunities, at its worst. What has it also been? An amazing opportunity to grow, be creative, experience new people, a wide variety of associations, industries, business practices, cities and countries. It's not been boring, and I hate boring. It's been challenging, fun and exciting.

I recently coached a senior vice-president for a large financial institution. The CEO asked me to. I felt nervous and excited, but decided early on I would do my best, I would guarantee confidentiality, I would establish trust. It turned out to be a wonderful experience. I asked him what he wished he'd known sooner in his career. His answer? I wish I'd learn to trust myself earlier.

I would have to say the same thing. Especially for us folk who like to succeed, who want to be improving and always bringing value to our work, it's so important to be less self-critical, to acknowledge our achievements and trust our own intuition, judgment, and good intentions.

In any initiative or opportunity pursuit there is an element of risk. Edward de Bono

---

I've been raising a kid on my own this whole time, since he was two. He's now 18, healthy, strong, a camp counsellor, swim instructor and lifeguard. I always said I would grow the business as I grew my kid. Well, he's off to University soon and it's time to put the marketing machine in motion. It's also time to go sit by a river and write poetry. I have both sides to my nature, the business drive and the artist's spirit. It's been my dilemma and my joy.

So I would also add, do the business your own way. If making a lot of money is your goal, stick to it and drive it hard. If growth and connection are what make you happy, put your intentions there. If you want to spend more time with your family, do it before it's no longer a choice. In the end, if you have clients who call you back, if you know and they know you've spoken well, if you have inspired and helped others, you will have more than enough money. You will have your integrity and a good name. That's success.

Randy E. Park, BSc, MEng

Thinking For Results™

- **A scientific curiousity...**
- **A concern for people...**
- **An expectation of progress...**
- **An embracing of reality...**
- **A mission to enhance thinking everywhere.**

Toronto, ON Canada
Phone: 416-703-9202
Fax: 416-703-9198
E-mail: rp@randypark.com
Web: www.randypark.com

RANDY PARK *is an engaging, thoughtful, understanding communicator.*

We're always thinking... but how effective is our thinking? Since 1986 Randy Park has trained and presented on fiber optics communications, dealing with technology. In the past six years he has collaborated in presenting diverse workshops on communicating with others, self understanding, conflict resolution, team building, and other topics.

In all these areas, from science to human nature, Randy observed that we rarely focussed on improving our own individual thinking process. Randy took on the challenge of creating simple but powerful tips, approaches, and strategies that can be used in a wide variety of situations. Through engaging, fun experiences, Randy helps people identify their own thought processing, so they can build on their strengths, think more effectively, and more often get the results they want.

Randy has published articles in print and electronically on both Thinking for Results and Fiber Optics. His book, **Thinking for Results**, *will be published in Fall 2002.*

• How I Got Started

I enjoy teaching. I have been teaching since my teenage years, when I taught sailing for several years as a summer job. (Like speaking, teaching sailing is lots of fun, but more work than it sounds!) I have also always been interested in physics and pursued first a Bachelor's then a Master's in degree, specializing in fibre optics. I started my company fifteen years ago with the intent of providing both consulting and training. People tell me I'm good at distilling complex information and explaining it in clear, easy to understand terms.

Eight or so years ago I "discovered" personal development. I learned that training and speaking give me all the key experiences that I must have in order to feel fulfilled. I also learned a lot about experiential learning, and created new techniques for teaching fibre optics. Training became my major focus and the majority of my business.

What I do today is important, for I am paying a day of my life for it. What I accomplish must be worthwhile, for the price is high. Unknown

---

My latent interest in learning about how people think and act was awakened. I trained with the company where I had taken the personal development courses, and led several of their programs.

Finally all the pieces started to fit together. My talents, abilities, research, and interests have gelled into keynotes and workshops on thinking more effectively. These are based on my own bent to think "rationally" tempered with the knowledge that thinking purely rationally or logically is almost impossible, since our past experiences, preferences and prejudices influence our thinking processes. For my clients in technology, this shows up in decision-making, troubleshooting, and problem solving, though most technical people have never looked at this aspect of their thought processes. Thus my fibre optics clients are also clients for practical workshops designed to help with everyday thinking.

• My Biggest Mistake

Several years ago, I did a joint presentation with a colleague at a conference. We had a fifteen-minute presentation with 35 mm slides and we alternated back and forth referring to the slides. After about three slides, the slide projector jammed. Our mistake: we tried to carry on. The problem was that our explanation relied heavily on the diagrams on the slides. As well, our timing got messed up.

Think like a man of action, act like a man of thought. Henri Bergson

---

Nowadays I always have a contingency plan. I now travel with my own laptop (usually a second one as well) and my own data projector—a set up I know will work. I arrive early and test everything. If diagrams are critical, I provide copies of the slides; in the worst case, I could work through the paper copies with them.

If a similar scenario happened again and the equipment was truly important to my presentation, I would stop. I'd acknowledge what had happened, assess if it could be fixed, and if so, wait for it to be fixed.

• My Best Success

My best success has come from customizing my material. Although I did this to some extent before CAPS, the emphasis that

CAPS members place on customization has hammered this home. I repeatedly found that I have won and kept clients because I insisted they tell me what they were looking for, and I listened and responded. In some cases, it was as simple as taking the topic list they provided and massaging it into a course outline. The reaction? "This is exactly what we are looking for!" Of course it is, they told me what they wanted. Yet the difference between others and me is that I listened.

> **The significant problems we have cannot be solved at the same level of thinking with which we created them.** Albert Einstein

In one case, a prospective client saw an outline for a public seminar I presented, and contacted the sponsoring organization to arrange the same seminar in-house. I knew that removing some material and adding other material would produce a better course for this company. Communicating through the third party to tune the content was a challenge, but it was worth it; I received excellent evaluations and went on to present dozens of seminars to this client. If I had delivered the "stock" presentation, I doubt they would have had me back.

Customization has several benefits, the biggest being that it clearly communicates to the client that their needs are the most important priority. We are determined to provide them with the most relevant content, no more and no less. The client knows that their time and money is being spent wisely and typically agrees to our recommended course length and seldom raises price objections.

> **The most erroneous stories are those we think we know best—and therefore never scrutinize or question.** Stephen Jay Gould

• What I Would Do Over

Although it hasn't been a straight line to get where I am today, I think most of the journey has been necessary. I have a financially successful training business in the niche of fibre optics, which I find interesting and enjoyable, and my newer programs in thinking more effectively, where I'm making some unique contributions. I've also had an enjoyable life along the way, with a reasonable balance between work, family, friends, and play.

If you think you can do a thing or think you can't do a thing, you're right. Henry Ford

---

Having said that, there are two things I would definitely do better if I had it all to do again. (These are things I still constantly remind myself.) The first is that I would plan more and set more precise goals. I realize that goals are not so much things to hit or miss, but guides for decision making. When my goals are clear, I can easily decide if an unusual project that comes up is something that fits in one way or another. In the past, there were many times where I would take a project just because it was business. Sometimes that is necessary to survive, but other times it is a distraction from achieving what is really important.

Take time to deliberate, but when the time for action has arrived, stop thinking and go in.
Napoleon Bonaparte

I would also set out a specific schedule for sales efforts. When I make the phone calls, I get more business, yet they are often the first things I set aside.

In summary, I would certainly become a speaker again. I know of no other work where I could develop so much personally as well as professionally. This development makes me not only a better speaker, but also a better person, and pays off in a life in which I am very fulfilled.

Tim R. Paulsen

T.R. Paulsen & Associates

Toronto, ON Canada
Phone: 416-465-0721
Fax: 416-463-3144
E-mail: tim@trpaulsen.com
Web: **www.trpaulsen.com**

TIM PAULSEN *is the principle of T. R. Paulsen & Associates, a training and consulting firm located in Toronto, Canada. He is the author of three books, numerous magazine articles and writes a monthly column for the National Credit News.*

For nearly 20 years, Tim has developed unique seminars, and then delivered the highly rated programs across North America. He has also presented successful programs in China, Malaysia and India.

Participants in his programs agree on two things about his programs:

1.) They are lively and fun

2.) They are rich in content, laden with practical suggestions that can be used right away.

Tim Paulsen is the past-president of the Toronto Chapter of CAPS (The Canadian Association of Professional Speakers), and serves on the current Board of Directors.

His subjects include:

- How to collect more money, quicker, ...and still keep your Customers
- 'Zen' Effective Business Writing – *How to do better, what we already do well!*

- Everything you need to know about e-mail, you've already learned from dating!
- Management of Time and Stress—*"But, I don't have time for a nervous breakdown!"*
- Customer Service—*Above & Beyond!*

• How I Got Started

The man was in his early sixties, weighed less than a microphone, and wore a perpetual frown on his pale face. He sat with his legs crossed in a single chair at the front of the room and it was obvious to those of us arriving in the hotel room in Pasedena that he was going to be our speaker for the next three days. *"Three days of this guy,"* I remember thinking to myself. *"Give me a break."*

I don't know who was listening, but "get a break" I got. At 9:00 a.m., Frank Hardesty uncoiled himself from his chair, uncrossed his arms, and put all twenty-seven of us into the palm of his hand. He held us there for the next three days.

If you would lift me, you must be on higher ground. Ralph Waldo Emerson

---

I was impressed by a great seminar and speaker and enchanted by the *apparent* life style of a seminar leader/speaker. Wow! One would get to travel, meet interesting people and, if Frank could be believed, be well paid for the effort. Back at our offices in Toronto, I developed our own in-house programs and delivered them within our company. I called Frank and told him I wanted to do more. He suggested a couple of things that I have heard since I came into CAPS. "Write some articles," Frank said. "When you have enough of them, they become chapters and then you have a book. *Once you have the book, you are an expert.*"

Well, there is a little more to it than that, but I did follow most of Frank's advice. In a short period of time, I was the author of a book about accounts receivable and contacted public seminar companies with my programs.

• My Biggest Mistake

Where to start? What to choose?

After wrestling with this one for several weeks, I decided, in no particular order, to tell you about my top three.

WHO IS THE BOSS?

When I was about as far away from home as possible, I made a mistake. A North American company contracted me to deliver a series of programs in China. There was a fair amount of development effort and time involved to deliver three *one-day* programs in a number of Chinese cities, including Shanghai and Beijing.

During one of the program days, I listened to some conflicting advice from two of the representatives from a company that traveled with me. There were a few *personal* issues involved as well, but what it really came down to was that I forgot who my client was when I attempted to deliver the program. I should have resolved the issues to my client's satisfaction. After all, the client is the boss.

It is okay to stumble because you are moving forward. Anonymous

---

FOLLOWING 'EXPERT' ADVICE:

One of our communication problems these days is that there is *so much* written about communications. As speakers and trainers, we get advice at our CAPS and NSA meetings, from books, the Internet, and magazines. A lot of the advice may be very good for us and our particular business, but some may not be an exact fit with what we do or our particular style. Some of it, even from an "expert" is simply bad advice.

I have acted too quickly on occasions, *hearing* something that sounds good and then buying a program or implementing a technique. A simple example is from an excellent book on marketing known as the "Guerrilla" series. It suggests that if you are in business, you need a business line and need to be listed in the telephone book. This is good advice for a certain *type* of business, but not a requirement for mine. As a result of acting on the advice, I converted an extra low cost residential line to a business line. I have a listing in the telephone book, for which I have never received a call, and pay substantially more each month for the privilege. In the total scheme of finance, it isn't a lot of money, but combine it with software or other services I've bought on "expert advice" (and didn't need) it adds up.

Never insult an alligator until you have crossed the river. Cordell Hull

---

KNOW WHEN TO WALK AWAY: KNOW WHEN TO RUN

I have strayed on occasions, when a client has called asking if I would deliver a keynote or a training session on a topic outside of the four subjects I cover (Accounts Receivable, Business Writing, Customer Service and Stress & Time Management). They were not as well received nor were they as much *fun* for me to deliver.

It isn't so much that I did a *bad* job. The seminars were at least *passable*, a few of them good, but they didn't measure up to what I would like to consider my usual standards.

I should have declined the invitations or to referred them to another speaker—a CAPS member if possible. It is tough to give up a fee, but the amount of money involved is not worth my speaking reputation. I will not stop *stretching* myself into other areas or topics on occasion, but I will make sure it is a topic that:

a)   I have an interest in and want to deliver

b)   I will doubly research, and keenly practice.

• My Best Success

Over the last few years, in addition to Canada and the United States, I have had the pleasure of delivering my programs in China, Malaysia and India. I would not have had *any* of the *International* bookings and certainly fewer in Canada and the U.S. if it weren't for my web site.

I respect faith, but doubt is what gives you an education. Wilson Mizner

---

The site has served me well for years and it continues to improve. On a snowy winter's day last year, we had Tom Antion as a guest speaker at CAPS Toronto. With his suggestions, my site now comes up as number one in several of the top search engines—including Lycos and Alta Vista.

True marketing doesn't ask what you want to sell, but what the customer wants to buy. Peter Drucker

---

• What I Would Do Over

I am *clever* but sometimes not so smart. I have never taken a public speaking course or had any *formal* training in the delivery of seminars or in public speaking. I've always felt that a maternal Irish ancestor kissed the blarney stone and *passed* me its legacy—the gift of gab. I've delivered a lot of programs while *thinking* on my feet, but even though there is some excitement in such a delivery, I doubt now that I gave the *best* of myself to the audience.

When you win, nothing hurts.
Joe Namath

If I had it to do over again, I would have taken more time to write my scripts and practice the delivery. This is not to say that my programs need to be delivered word for word, but I am certain if I took careful time to document, review, and test, I would leave the very best impression—*every time.*

The trials and tribulations of life bring each of us our share of disappointments. Yet, they also leave behind a greater sense of understanding, toleration and sympathy for others—something we never felt to the same extent when we were younger.
Marianne Williamson

Richard Peterson, CSP

The Presentation Coach

Coaching professionals to become powerful presenters!

- **Executive Presentation Coaching**
- **Advanced Executive Sales Coaching**
- **Media and Interview Skills**
- **Executive Image Consulting**
- **Speech Writing and Presentation Development**

Thornhill, ON Canada
Phone: 905-760-9072
E-mail: richard@passociates.com
Web: www.passociates.com

RICHARD PETERSON *specializes in coaching professionals to become more powerful presenters. Richard earned the prestigious CSP designation (Certified Sales Professional) allowing him to coach sales professionals to reach greater success through powerful presentation skills. His supportive coaching approach is designed to nurture individuals at a pace that benefits them.*

Richard's diverse client base, from corporate executives to professional athletes, attests to his tremendous wealth of experience. His presentation and coaching expertise, honed during consumer product launches, corporate reviews, training and sales conferences, media appearances, and university lectures, evolved from his corporate years of Marketing, Sales and International Sponsorship Negotiation.

Serving on the Board of the Canadian Association of Profession/al Speakers and authoring the program, "Avoid the 5 Biggest Presentation Mistakes Professionals Make!" has led to students and recent business articles refer to him as Canada's Presentation Coach.

Readers interested in receiving Presentation Tips directly from Richard may e-mail him at: richard@passociates.com or www.passociates.com. He will share five additional Presentation Tips with professionals committed to becoming more powerful presenters.

Speaking is a Business?...now you tell me!

• How I Got Started

I SPENT TWENTY YEARS IN A CORPORATE ROLE AND IT WAS BEYOND ME THAT SPEAKING COULD QUALIFY AS A BUSINESS!

Many evenings, after a long day of meetings, my employer often reminded me that speaking was "part of the job." Another "part" involved taking on "Special Projects."

Presentation Tip

PREPAREDNESS: Be prepared to expand on a presentation point when the audience reaction is positive for greater impact and to demonstrate your natural expertise in the subject.

Richard Peterson

Eventually, a project came along that involved organizing a major Canadian Sales Conference. This conference was different. Corporate downsizing had again taken its toll and this audience was made up of the survivors. The meeting planner suggested hiring an outsource speaker. Reluctantly, I agreed, but wondered about the speaker's day job. What could that be? Then I realized a startling truth; speaking was his day job!

I watched and listened with skepticism as the speaker opened the conference. Imagine an audience feeling pain, fear and even personal relief because many of their colleagues were not in attendance that fateful morning. I vaguely remember the speaker's words as I watched the individual audience members attentive to every phrase, but I do remember the mesmerizing silence.

Post-conference, I took part in conversations with individuals who recalled how that speaker had helpfully impacted their attitudes. Weeks later, over lunch, I met with this man to pass on our very positive observations. I can recall staring down into the bottom of my cup as I swirled the last bits of coffee. I envied his influence and the fact that his words mattered. Suddenly, my hectic, frenetic corporate lifestyle held very little meaning to me.

Note to Self: Make speaking my day job!

• My Biggest Mistake

INTRODUCING A NEW ELEMENT INTO A PRESENTATION ONLY HOURS BEFORE SHOW TIME!

I was about to make a presentation in Orlando, Florida. I had every detail in place, that is until only hours before show time, I decided to introduce a new element involving theatrical costuming and props. Imagine for a moment, a large audience, a techno light and sound show and a tall, island stage. Moments into the presentation, while I fumbled with new props, I created a move that involved traveling around the platform. Then it happened. How do I put this? I ran out of stage. Spread-eagle as a skydiver, I tumbled backwards over the rear lip of the stage and disappeared from view into a tangled octopus of sound cords and wires just behind the platform. Not missing the moment, I leapt to my feet and loudly proclaimed, "That's my point! If you insist on going to the edge—know what's on the other side—it makes for a softer landing!"

The audience roared and applauded to what they thought was a planned delivery. I didn't have the heart to confess I simply fell off the stage!

Note to Self: Go to the edge knowing what's on the other side. It makes for a softer landing

• My Best Success

**BEING HONEST WITH MYSELF, I REALIZED I WAS ALONE.
I NEEDED HELP AND I NEEDED HELP FAST!**

Corporate deadlines have comfort and built in flexibility. If I sometimes missed a deadline, I efficiently created a new one. My career was different now. For a speaker, deadline comes at the end of the month - every nickel, dime and penny end of the month. If ever I forgot, then my bank manager was an expert at reminding me.

Presentation Tip

SIMPLICITY IN VISUALS: Carefully chosen, easy to read visuals will show your audience advance planning, creativity and thinking that weaves its way throughout your presentation.

Richard Peterson

Yet, my years of business training didn't seem to help. I thought back to the speaker I hired and asked how he did it. His advice? Get involved with other speakers! Make mistakes and learn from those mistakes! The advice seemed simple enough. Because of it, I launched into a vertical learning curve. My immediate goal was to make as many mistakes as I could in the shortest time possible. Why wait twenty-five years over a speaking career to learn from mistakes I could make all at once?

When I was welcomed into the Canadian Association of Professional Speakers (they probably weren't aware of my mistakes philosophy), I watched timidly from a distance, and then volunteered for everything they needed volunteers for. Next, sourcing speakers for monthly meetings as CAPS Program Chair gave me access to knowledge from some of the best speakers in the business. Finally, a leadership position on the CAPS Board validated all the knowledge I had gained in a short period of time.

The exchange, support and friendships gained from the organization brought clarity to my past business experience and allowed me to focus on the development of my new career.
I realized speaking is not only a wonderful business, but also a new way of life.

Note to Self: Making mistakes leads to growth and lifelong learning

• What I Would Do Over

OPEN MY MIND TO NEW THINKING SOONER

I realized I held a narrow view of the definition of the business world. Years of business training led me to believe there was a single way of doing things. The corporate workplace was enormous and at the same time isolating. Some projects were led single handedly with very little support, encouragement or clarity.

In the beginning, I resisted the coaching offered by my speaker colleagues. It felt alien and invasive at times. I became suspicious and thought 'There there must be something in it for them!' Besides, what else was there to learn after the twenty years of training and experience that I had?

The giving nature of my speaking colleagues has helped me develop my nurturing style of coaching with clients—and that's what's in it for them to help me become better. Period.
One more thing, I would have paid more attention in accounting class.

Note to Self: Accept previous life and work experiences and welcome the ideas and support of others.

Presentation Tip

INFLUENTIAL FINISH: Your powerful final words may be the most remembered; the finish will hold more influence with the audience if met with conclusion moving to timely action.

Richard Peterson

Real Recognition™

London, ON Canada
Phone: 519-685-0664
Fax: 519-685-0819
E-mail: Roy@RealRecognition.com
Web: **www.RealRecognition.com**

Roy Saunderson

ROY SAUNDERSON *specializes in helping leaders and managers in attracting, recognizing and keeping key people.*

Since 1994 Roy's programs and consulting have helped his clients increase productivity, purpose and profits by ensuring their key people are motivated, loyal, and not lost to the competition. Some of his clients include Bell Canada, Canada Post, Royal Bank, 3M Canada, Siemens Canada, along with government ministries and agencies, and various professional and trade associations.

He is the author of the book How To Focus On Success! *and* 101 Ways To Give EVERYDAY Real Recognition, *along with many articles in business, professional and trade journals and magazines.*

Roy's sessions draw upon the participation of his audiences to remind them of the importance of what it takes to really keep employees motivated and stay with their organization. His ability to help people implement his ideas after his presentations has become a hallmark tradition of his work in giving people Real Recognition™.

• How I Got Started

WITH A LITTLE HELP FROM MY FRIENDS

Have you ever noticed friends struggling with something and you simply strode over to help them? That's how I got into the speaking business.

Sometime around 1986 or so, I was working in a rehabilitation hospital as a speech-language pathologist. It was there I noticed that my colleagues in physiotherapy were stressed to the point of burning out. I had to ask myself why *I* wasn't stressed. After jotting some points into a basic format I visited my friends and said, "I'd like to help. Would you like me to give you a lunch-time presentation one day on how to overcome stress?"

They were *so* grateful. Not only did it go well as a presentation, but also their manager talked to my boss about what a positive difference it had made on morale and performance. Next thing you know it was "Nurses Week" and they wanted a presentation too!

After a couple of public seminars on stress management to healthcare professionals, my business was launched.

When you follow your bliss... doors will open
where you would not have thought there would
be doors; and where there wouldn't be a door
for anyone else. Joseph Campbell

• My Biggest Mistake

YA GOTTA KNOW WHEN TO FOLD 'EM

I will never forget this one. Topic-wise, when I started speaking part-time, I was a generalist. I was eager to accept any business that came my way. Money seemed to be my sole motivation. Big mistake!

One request came to speak for a rural area association of school principals. They wanted a presentation on "humour in the workplace." I rationalized the "workplace issues" I assumed they needed to resolve. I can be quite funny during my presentations. However, this was before I became proficient in doing background research and preparation. My topics were not well enough prepared for the immediate audience.

Well, I was the evening speaker after several daytime educator-specific and dry presentations. Then came supper. Then came the drinks.

I was next.

Failure is only the opportunity to begin again more intelligently. Henry Ford

---

The rest was history. The presentation was okay. I had researched all kinds of jokes to go with the points that were intended to be educational and humourous. Apparently, their expectations differed from mine.

They probably wanted a comedian. I did not fit the bill. It was one time I wanted to get off the platform quickly. My jokes flopped. Their faces became sullen. It was a HUGE revelation for me.

A few days later, the oganizers acknowledged that what they had asked for *was not what they really wanted*. Apologies were given on both sides. And I vowed NEVER to speak on humour in the workplace again or on any topic where I didn't excel.

• My Best Success

CAME FROM A 3-YEAR OLD

I remember my first ever showcase presentation as a novice speaker for a speakers' bureau in Toronto. I was very nervous and over-rehearsed for my twenty-minute presentation that afternoon. My topic was on "Communicating From Within," but most of it was drawn from material of other people.

Like most speakers there that day, we sat in on other speakers' sessions. Imagine hearing a well-known sports commentator using a joke in the middle of his presentation that was going to be YOUR closing story!

I sat there numbed. I went blank. I remember dawdling over lunch and not really listening to my table company. I couldn't think of a single story. I had NOTHING to replace the joke I had for my closing lines.

When in doubt, say a little prayer!

Being a new speaker and the only one during two concurrent sessions, I was in the smaller room with slightly more people than the room could hold. But who was that at the back of the room? Yes, it was the famous basketball coach and sports celebrity, Jack Donohue. In MY session!

Communication is more than a sharing of words. It is the wise sharing of emotions, feelings, and concerns. It is the sharing of oneself totally.

Marvin J. Ashton

If there was ever a time I had to "communicate from within" this was it. I was nervous, but inspiration kicked in about how to close.

I told the audience of meeting planners and speakers that I was going to make a prediction. I paused… It may have looked extremely professional. Finally, I was prepared for what I would say.

I told them that when I got home that night I knew that my 3-old daughter would come running to the door, shouting "Daddy! Daddy!" and then would give me a great big hug. The story continued. I concluded with a quote saying, "Communication is more than a sharing of words. It is the wise sharing of emotions, feelings, and concerns. It is the sharing of oneself totally. Let us all communicate like a 3-year old."

Sometimes we get stuck with "three to get ready, three to get ready" Rosita Perez

---

Within a week, a meeting planner who had attended that session hired me. Six months later at the event, I finally met her face to face. Just when I was about to present, she commented, "I hope you don't do what you did when I heard you at the showcase session."

Oh, oh. What did I do then that she doesn't want me to do now? You can guess I was anxious not to make the same mistake for this paid event. Instead of relaying some expected flaw she said, "You made me cry with your closing story."

I have learned that the best material comes from our own lives. The greatest stories are from the ordinary experiences we go through or observe in others. Never again did I rely on stories or jokes from a book. Never again will I be left hanging because someone else had stolen my lines.

• What I Would Do Over

OH, BOY! IF ONLY…

1. I would have gone full-time into speaking sooner, rather than waiting for the elusive "secure moment."

2. I would have written a book(s) and created products right away.

3. I would have asked for specific marketing advice and coaching right from the beginning.

4. I would have focused more on making a business than "just" the love of speaking.

Jean Sinden

Leveraging Performance

Oro Station, ON Canada
Phone: 705-733-0582
E-mail: jean@jeansinden.com
Web: **www.jeansinden.com**

JEAN SINDEN *is a Speaker, Strategic Planner, Corporate Trainer and Consultant. The common theme through Jean's work is the encouragement of members of organizations to be entrepreneurial.*

Jean developed her expertise in these areas over more than a twenty-year career in the private and public sectors. She has delivered over 1,000 programs throughout Canada and in the United States, working with multinational and independently owned businesses as well as not-for-profit and government organizations.

She was co-founder and financial manager of a charter fishing business on Vancouver Island and was also part owner and business manager for an electrical contracting firm.

She has served as president of the Toronto Chapter of CAPS and of the Greater Barrie Chamber of Commerce. She is an elected member of the Governing Council of the Ontario Chamber of Commerce.

Jean is regarded as an industry expert in assisting businesses and organizations to grow and prosper in the increasingly complex environment in which they operate.

• How I Got Started

I was six years old when I won my first oratory contest. The applause, smiles and laughter are still with me today. Unfortunately there is little call for six-year-old professional speakers so I continued with the "experience" of growing up. I started and ran businesses in electrical contracting and tourism and took the path to being an accountant. Then the speaking bug re-entered my life.

I ventured into politics and was elected as a school trustee. This reinforced my love of standing up in front of audiences and speaking.

I decided that if I wanted to make a living as a speaker I had to hone my skills and find something to speak about. I sought out the position where I could accomplish both these goals and get paid at the same time. Eventually I was hired as a seminar leader with a financial institution dealing with small business and I was thrown into the fire... designing presentations and training materials and delivering and facilitating training sessions.

My success in this role resulted in my being promoted to a management role on the other side of the desk. I hired speakers and developed a network of speakers and trainers for seminars and conferences. I also continued to deliver seminars on business topics and the same time, was training in strategic planning.

It's never too late to become what you might have been. George Elliot

---

In one of those common twists of living we often share, my personal life was altered. I, a firm believer in (as the licence plates say) "Beautiful British Columbia," moved to the "dreaded"... Ontario.

I knew practically no one in Ontario, but I did have my love of speaking, a core of business training topics that I had delivered, and my own experiences in business. In addition, I had that training in strategic planning. I launched my business on the combination of training and facilitation of strategic plans with the thought that each would complement the other.

There are no mistakes, no coincidences, all events are blessings given to us to learn from.
Elizabeth Kübler-Ross

In order to gain clients, my first challenge was to become known in the "new" marketplace. It was a no-brainer that I had to get out into the business community "quickly". I sought out the local Chamber of Commerce, community college and key people that I needed to meet. This is how I spent my first couple of years in business. These contacts led to my becoming president of the local chamber and also to being sought to train and speak for various events. I wrote columns in local business publications and had a local cable TV segment called "Business and You."

All of these efforts led to recognition and demand for my services. My career in the speaking business was off and running.

• My Biggest Mistake

MY BIGGEST MISTAKE OFF THE PLATFORM

Having the belief that a good product, well delivered with satisfied customers would equate to business success and growth.

I began to rely too much on others to call me. I was busy and making good money. I wasn't doing the networking and marketing that had previously worked so well for me.

The motivation and desire I had initially to become credible and established began to wane once I had achieved my original goal. I was comfortable that repeat business and word of mouth referrals would keep the business growing but instead it *stalled.*

It was far more difficult to restart from a stall then it would have been to keep building on the momentum I had originally developed.

MY BIGGEST MISTAKE ON THE PLATFORM

I had delivered hundreds of presentations and was invited to participate in a Speakers' Showcase. Confident, I got there early to network and hear the other speakers, but during the build-up to my allotted time, the enormity of the occasion crept into my mind. These people could actually hire me for high paying engagements, but others ahead of me on the platform were the competition—and they were *good.*

When one is a stranger to oneself, then one is estranged from others too. Anne Morrow Lindburgh

---

I forgot the basics of presenting: breathe deeply and have a glass of water near by. When I started speaking, I had no saliva and could hardly mouth the words of my presentation. This had never happened to me before and there was no recovering. I can still feel the shock and disappointment of that day.

• My Best Success

I have been adamant from the beginning; I was developing a business, not a hobby. Like businesses everywhere, I have had to practice continuous improvement.

In presenting myself as a business I established a fee structure that reflected the experience and talent that I bring to my clients. I have not been willing to accept any offer in order to get the work.

In practicing continuous improvement, I have developed new areas of expertise and have worked to keep material current and relevant.

I research and learn about my clients' (or prospective clients') industry and their business. A little knowledge about the firm and industry goes a long way towards building credibility both in the initial negotiation phase as well as the actual presentation.

I work on my craft, I attend professional development sessions and belong to professional associations.

We don't see things as they are, we see them as we are. Anaïs Nin

---

My best success has been surviving. This is a direct result of my perseverance and commitment to this business. Some projects that I have been selected for are a result of my being established since 1989.

I am involved in CAPS and also maintain my volunteer role with the Ontario Chamber of Commerce. Credibility and visibility are so important, particularly when seeking out projects with middle and senior managers.

I entered this business with the knowledge and savvy required to thrive. I am able to draw on my experience and wisdom of how to manage and succeed.

• What I Would Do Over

Spend more of my effort on developing speaking opportunities and aligning with the conference market. This would include focusing more on platform skills as well as developing and delivering keynotes.

Apply more of what I was learning from the seasoned pros at CAPS and to ask for help from others. For support and guidance, I'd get to know other speaking professionals sooner. This can be a lonely business and we need to take the same approach we would if we were in a new job or organization.

Without information you cannot take responsibility; with information you can't avoid it. Jan Carlzon

---

The corporate training environment is a great place to add depth and content. Over the past decade, training and facilitation skills have become core competencies in many environments. The value given to experience and flexibility with both content and practical application is not considered as important as it once was.

Keep in closer contact with clients and be more proactive in providing them with ongoing solutions. This includes using the tools of technology and taking more of a systems approach to the marketing function.

Work with a sales representative so that I would have a constant profile in the marketplace, which would help to lessen the "*feast or famine*" cycles of this business. I would also benefit from having an agent to negotiate on my behalf.

Tom Stoyan, HoF

Canada's Sales Coach

TOM STOYAN
SEMINARS

Woodbridge, ON   Canada
Phone: 416-410-4441
E-mail:
TomStoyan@CanadasSalesCoach.com
Web: **www.CanadasSalesCoach.com**

TOM STOYAN: *Hall of Fame Professional*

Tom Stoyan has served as coach to sales and management professionals for more than fifteen years. He coaches professionals to get the best out of themselves and others.

A former college professor, he is the founding president of the Ontario Chapter of the National Speakers Association that later became the Canadian Association of Professional Speakers (CAPS) and is a past director of the Association of Independent Consultants. Tom was the first inductee into the Canadian Speaking Hall of Fame!

Known as Canada's Sales Coach, he is author of five books:
- Sell More...101 Ideas To Increase Sales Now!
- The Power of Networking!
- The Do's & Don'ts of Telemarketing! *(with Elayne Nusbam)*
- Networking for Results *(with Michael J. Hughes)*
- Managing the Networking Process *(with Michael J. Hughes)*

His Sell More *book has been endorsed by more sales trainers, associations and sales professionals than any other book of its kind. His Networking booklet is published by the largest sales association in Canada. Tom's coaching book is expected to be released early in the New Year.*

Tom's sales & marketing strategies have resulted in doing work with the teams of such diverse groups as IBM, Rogers, Air Canada, Hallmark, KPMG, Merck, AT&T, GE, Newcourt Credit Group, Scotiabank, Freightliner, Sheraton Hotels, Profit Magazine, Avid Media, Canada Post and the Royal Bank of Canada. He has completed a national tour of his program, "Sales & the CEO". Shortly after, he was invited back for his "Executive Coaching Skills & Strategies" program.

He has been invited to present at numerous corporations and associations including: the Canadian Society of Association Executives, Ontario Society of Training & Development, Western Business School Club of Toronto, Canadian Association of Financial Planners and the York Technology Association. He was the only presenter invited back to speak to Profit *Magazine's Hottest Startups two years in a row.*

Tom specializes in coaching professionals to improve their ability in acquiring and retaining more clients. His programs are highly customized and focused on helping individuals break through the barrier of "knowing" to "doing". His programs are about doing better vs. knowing more!

• How I Got Started

Having had a very successful sales background, resulted in one of my clients asking if I would explain to his team what I did that worked so well for me. My supplier heard about the presentation and asked me to share the same with his new sales agents. Shortly after I heard of and then attended my first NSA convention.

I knew if I was going to be successful in a new career, I needed to surround myself with folks already doing it.

The shoemaker makes a good shoe because he makes nothing else. Emerson

---

• My Biggest Mistake

As the founder of the first professional speakers association in Toronto, I ran the meetings of the Ontario Speakers Association. The first two years I was in front of mostly folks like myself who wanted to become a professional speaker. But we were fortunate to have Allan Simmons and Warren Evans (both members of our Hall of Fame) support our association from the very beginning. As professional speakers they had already mastered techniques we were just beginning to experience. Alan's wife, Susan approached me on more than one occasion with an excellent suggestion. One which would have raised my professional image. I was a slow learner. I didn't think I needed what she suggested. I should have known better.

Some folks are wise and some are otherwise.

Tobias George Smollet

I have long known the power of a professional image. From my television days as both a producer and host, I learned the importance of looking the part. I knew about good grooming: about getting a hair cut before it needs it; nails clipped (I even remember to cut my eye brows as well the hair growing from my ears & nose!)

Although all of that is important, I was still missing an important part of the picture. It wasn't the eye I failed to please. It was the ear. You see I never really learned how to use a hand held microphone. And because of that, I refused to use one early in my career. I thought the issue was since they could hear me, there was no need to use a mic. Boy, was I wrong. Because of that I didn't sound as professional as I not only could have but should have.

The use of a microphone presents a professional image that can't be duplicated without it. It allows one to play with the voice, to affect the mood and in a meaningful way, impact the message.

Much of the audience would miss my throw away lines. Those after thoughts (or so the audience liked to think) that added humour or broke the tension from an emotional point. The after-lines by using contrast would add the emotional impact to what I had just said.

If you think you can't learn anything from a fellow member, you likely aren't listening or watching closely enough.

• My Best Success

My best success came from.... looking for opportunities to live my life's philosophy

The philosophy that got me here can be summed up in two sentences. *Don't tell me I can't do it. Tell me what I need to do to make it happen!* From having spent two years in the second grade to being told in the eighth grade, I was the worst speller in the county, this philosophy has served me well.

Don't tell me I can't do it. Tell me what I need to do to make it happen.

Tom Stoyan

This business calls on you and I to find something important to share with the world. That something is in you. Most of us spend much of our life looking for it outside of our self. As a result of our experiences, we develop a life philosophy. We develop beliefs about our world and how we want to play in it. We develop our perspective. For me, being told no, didn't make sense. This included:

"You can't take the five year program in Ontario, you are going to fail anyway, but by taking the four year program you won't make me look so bad." said my principal.

"You can't go to university, you don't have the background or the discipline to succeed."

"You can't go to the US to school. You don't have any money."

I didn't listen to them. Instead I put my life's philosophy into action and made a commitment to life-long learning. What did it get me? It allowed me to earn a full scholarship at Syracuse University. It allowed me to get my first teaching job in 1973 in a recession when I was told there were no teaching jobs available. It allowed me to become one of the youngest professors at State University in New York.

Every person is the architect of their own fortune.

English Proverb

Living my life's philosophy resulted in reading over 300 books in sales and coaching. It gave me the competence to work with some of Canada's biggest and best companies. It expanded my confidence to coach over 150 CEOs and presidents in both their selling and coaching skills.

Living my life's philosophy resulted in becoming a Super Elite Air Canada customer.

Living my life's philosophy paid for my Jaguars, Porsches and a Lexus SC400 (my favourite car).

Living my life's philosophy resulted in having my first book endorsed by 34 professionals including Brain Tracy, Nido Quebein and Mark Victor Hansen (who wrote the preface).

• What I Would Do Over

Give more free talks, more often, earlier in my career.

Don't be fooled. You don't speak about something. You share a part of you. Speaking is a way to discover what "it" is for you. When you discover what that is, this business will get into you. When you leverage it, you will accelerate your success in this business. You will make mistakes along the way. The sooner you recognize them, the sooner to get to profit from them.

Change
Courage
Connectivity

Phone: 416-533-1532
E-mail: linda@lindatarrant.com
Web: **www.lindatarrant.com**

Linda Tarrant, CSP, HoF

LINDA TARRANT *was born to the speaking business. Her grandmother once said that she could "talk a sign post out of the ground". She took that as a compliment and has been speaking ever since. She is originally from Kentucky and has lived in Canada since 1974.*

Linda is a Certified Speaking Professional (CSP) and a member of the Canadian Speaking Hall of Fame (HoF). She is currently (2002) the President Elect of the Canadian Association of Professional Speakers.

Linda is a partner in TOC Consulting, Inc. and is a master facilitator and change agent. Linda brings skills, tools and practical techniques to help individuals and organizations come to grips with a transforming world. Her positive and powerful message is enhanced through storytelling and a wonderful sense of humour. Linda speaks on Change, Courage and Connectivity.

• How I Got Started

I lost my job. I was out of work with no idea what to do next. I was living in Lethbridge, Alberta and winter was approaching, so I moved to Vancouver. Even though I was unemployed, I knew enough to find a warm place to look for a job. I quickly contacted several of my friends who lived in town to say hello and tell them about my plight. Ian Percy was one of those friends. He took me to lunch (after all, I was out of work) and suggested that I do some training and consulting work with him until I could find a job. I've been looking for a job ever since, but I've never found one that I like better than this one. So here I am.

One of the difficulties in bringing about change in an organization is that you must do so through the persons who have been most successful in that organization, no matter how faulty the system or organization is. To such persons, you see, it is the best of all possible organizations because look who was selected by it and look who succeeded most with it. Yet, these are the very people through whom we must bring about improvements.

George Washington

But it wasn't really that simple. I didn't just get into the business and stay there. My business took a dramatic turn as a result of the first NSA Winter Workshop that I attended. I went because it was in Bermuda, but I didn't leave the hotel for three days. I could have been in Siberia. I was totally absorbed.

During that workshop, I was struck by two concepts that made me take a totally different view of my business. The first seemed so simple, but it hit me like a ton of bricks. I heard participants introduce themselves as "professional speakers." I didn't even know there was such an animal. I had always thought of myself as a trainer, facilitator and consultant, but certainly not as a "professional speaker." When I thought about what that meant to me, I realized that I was facing my next professional challenge. It was time for me to get into the keynoting business. It was the next logical step but I hadn't realized it before that workshop. I was terrified! The first time I introduced myself as a "Professional Speaker", I felt like the ultimate imposter. I was shocked when no one laughed or questioned my newly chosen career. They just asked, "So, what do you speak about?" Then came my next great learning.

Does all this change make people feel insecure? Of course. But anybody who recognizes what is going on in this world and isn't somewhat insecure, I would argue, is not awake. And I think the biggest enemy of progress is happy talk. You need to tell people that if we do not change, and change fundamentally, we are going out of business. And that will create insecurity. The trick is to turn that insecurity into constructive tension.

Mike Walsh (former CEO, Tenneco)

The second concept struck me during Joe Callaway's concurrent session at that same workshop. He talked about his "elevator speech." That was how he explained what he did in the time it took an elevator to get between two floors. I was mortified. It took me five minutes to explain what I did for a living and by then people's eyes were starting to glaze over. I realized that I had no focus for my work. I needed to figure out what business I was in if I was ever going to be really successful. Well, I've figured it out, at least for now. When someone asks what I do, I tell them that I'm a professional speaker and facilitator and I speak on Change, Courage and Connectivity. Quite often the person asks me to tell them more about at least one of those things. That's my opportunity to create a relationship and maybe even book an engagement.

So, how did I get into the business? I was lucky enough to lose my job, know Ian Percy and go to a NSA Winter Workshop.

• My Biggest Mistake

Unfortunately, this is an easy question to answer but such a difficult one to change. It always happens when I don't listen to the little voice inside of me that is screaming, "Don't take this job! It's not right. You're going to regret this." I usually know when it's wrong early on in the interview. I often try to get out of it. But, it's so hard for me to say "no", even when I hear that voice.

One thing that I'm learning (it's an on-going process) is that I must be true to myself and to the people in the audience. If I don't think it's right for me or the client, I have to say no. So my biggest mistake is getting on the platform when I know I'm not the right fit.

• My Best Success

For me it's been the people in my life. For starters, I was fortunate enough to come from a loving family that gave me unconditional positive regard. They are positive, hopeful and happy. I once told my mother that I've made a great living out of telling people what she told me for free. I really can't help it if I have a positive attitude, hope for the future and the desire to celebrate and have as much fun as possible. It's genetic.

155

Then there were Ian Percy and Jane O'Callaghan. Ian got me into the business and continually mentored, challenged and believed in me. I wouldn't be here without him. When Jane and I became partners in TOC Consulting, my/our business really took off. I would never have been so successful working on my own. We share a common philosophy but we each bring different skills and perspectives to our work and life in general. More importantly, I would never have traveled the world and had so many wonderful and terrifying experiences without her zest for adventure.

It's hard to plot a rational course in an irrational environment. So don't be blinded by reason or logic. Be ever vigilant. Take a nap and you could wake up like Rip Van Winkle! Watts Wacker, The 500 Year Delta

---

I've become a better person, speaker and facilitator because of all the wonderful people who have wanted me to be a success and have helped me along the way. My advice is to watch who you hang around with. Make sure some of them push you to think differently and to become more than you ever thought you could be. That being said, hang around with people who love you for who you are and not what you do.

Then give back as generously to other people who come into your life.

In order for an organization to succeed, it must be resilient, flexible and selective in an unpredictable world, and its planners must be intelligent, visionary and brave. R.E. Wilhelm, EXXON

• What I Would Do Over

I just can't imagine changing anything because that might have changed everything. And then where would I be? I have made many mistakes and errors of judgment in my life and I have had tons of wonderful experiences and I have learned and changed as a result of each one. I know that I have lost opportunities that came my way when I was not ready or willing to take them. I'll never know where they might have led me. But I do know where I've ended up so far and that I could not be more thankful.

Prepare for eternity: Tidy up your room.

Ashleigh Brilliant

The only thing I might have changed was to get involved with CAPS and NSA earlier in my career. It certainly would have accelerated my learning about the speaking business and increased my network of speaking friends. But, actually, I may not have been in a state of readiness any earlier in my career. So, I think I'll just be grateful for everything that has come my way and hope that I will be as fortunate in the back half of my life and that I use what I've been given as best I can.

Motivation and inspiration make difficult things seem more possible. Action makes them happen!

Linda Tarrant

Harold Taylor, CSP, HoF

Taylor On Time

Harold Taylor Time Consultant Inc.

Newmarket, ON Canada
Phone: 905-853-9328
Fax: 905-853-9390
E-mail: harold@taylorontime.com
Web: www.taylorontime.com

HAROLD TAYLOR, *president of Harold Taylor Time Consultants Inc. has been speaking, writing and conducting training programs on the topic of effective time management for over 25 years. He has written 15 books, including a Canadian bestseller, Making Time Work For You. He has developed over 50 time management products that have sold in 38 countries around the world. His monthly Time Management Report has been published for twenty-two years and he has had over 200 articles accepted for publication.*

A past director of the National Association of Professional Organizers, Harold received their Founder's Award in 1999 for outstanding contributions to the organizing profession. He received the CSP (Certified Speaking Professional) designation in 1987 from the National Speakers Association. In 1998 the Canadian Association of Professional Speakers inducted him into the Canadian Speaking Hall of Fame. And in 2001, he received the Founder's Award from the Professional Organizers in Canada. The award has been named in his honor.

Prior to his speaking career, Harold held management positions in industry for twelve years and taught business subjects for eight years at Humber College in Toronto. He has been an entrepreneur for over thirty years, incorporating four companies during that time, all of which are still operating successfully. Since 1981, when he incorporated the time management company, he has presented over 2000 workshops, speeches and keynotes on the topic of time and life management.

• How I Got Started

I eased into the speaking business gradually. Having overcome my fear of speaking during my eight-year tenure as a college teacher, I started sponsoring a few management workshops on the side. This eventually opened the door to in-house presentations, then speeches, and finally keynotes. When I realized that with a little effort I could make money doing something I love, I went full-time into the business.

• My Biggest Mistake

I made many mistakes on the platform, and still do; but the most persistent and damaging one was acting as though a speech were simply a condensed workshop. Consequently I tried to cram a full-day workshop into a half-hour speech by talking faster and hitting the highlights. I felt compelled to tell the audience everything I knew regardless of my time limit. It took many years before I discovered that only 10 percent of your success depends on what you say and 90 percent depends on how you say it

• My Best Success

I learned early in my speaking career that you couldn't be an expert in everything. The world of knowledge is just too big and our time on earth too short. I was fortunate to have specialized in one area, time management, and to maintain my focus by writing a mission statement. This kept me from being sidetracked by enticing opportunities that had nothing to do with my chosen topic. My mission is simply:

> "To help individuals and organizations manage their time, achieve their goals and manage their lives as effectively as possible through workshops, presentations, products, publications and personal example."

This mission statement, along with my vision to become the top time management authority in the country, allowed me to set annual goals that included self-development as well as products, bookings and promotion.

• **What I Would Do Over**

If I were to sing Frank Sinatra's song, "I Did It My Way", it would come out, *Regrets, I have a few hundred, but then again too many to mention here.* But here are a few:

- That I didn't accumulate some start-up money before launching my first business. It could have taken at least 5 years off the start-up stage.

- That I didn't go with first-class promotional materials right from the start. It's hard to project success with a hand-made brochure.

- That I didn't spend more time promoting the programs I offered as opposed to spending all my effort promoting myself. Then it would have been easier to delegate the instruction to others, and more acceptable to my clients.

- That it took me eight years to build up my self-confidence enough to quit my job and go full-time in my business.

- That I didn't outsource more jobs and spend less time in areas that were not my area of expertise.

- That I wasn't aggressive enough to ask for testimonials and referrals even when I didn't charge for my services.

- That I under rated the value of my services and undervalued the cost of my time.

- That I initially took on assignments that were beyond my area of expertise simply because they paid well.

- That I spent too many hours per day on the company as a result of perfectionism and the bad habit of trying to do everything myself.

- That I was too proud to ask my peers for help.

- That I talked more than I listened.

- That I didn't send thank you notes to every client and follow up with them on a regular basis.

Wise men talk because they have something to say; fools because they have to say something. Plato

---

But then again, there are several things I have been thankful for. Among them:

- That I specialized early in my speaking career.

- That I wrote a book early in my career and went with a publishing company for the extra credibility as opposed to self-publishing.

- That I didn't skimp when sending a promotion package to a prospect enquiring about a program.

- That I had specific goals to aim for each year.

- That I was willing to take risks by trying new things.

- For having started with low cost and free seminars to the business community.

- That I developed products early in my speaking career.

- That I sold products at the back of the room at my seminars and keynotes.

- That I spent more money on books than I did on food and clothes.

  And finally, I still have hopes:

- That I never use age as an excuse for not starting something new.

- That I never forget where I came from or the people who helped me along the way.

- That the future will always be more appealing than the past.

- That I never stop learning.

- That I never run out of ideas before I run out of life.

CAPS
PROFESSIONAL TRAINERS,
FACILITATORS AND KEYNOTERS

Francis J. Theriault, ATM, PM

Beyond Selling ...Excelling!™

- TTS Performance Consultants
- Theriault Training Seminars
- WORDsmithing Professional Writing and Editing Services
- Business and Corporate Communication HR Consultants

Whitby, ON Canada
Phone: 905-571-7939
Toll Free: 866-571-7939
E-mail: francis@theriault.ca
Web: **www.theriault.ca**

FRANCIS J. THERIAULT *is a popular Conference Speaker and Retreat leader. With over 25 years of successful experience in Sales, Marketing, Management, and Training, Francis continues to be a popular Conference Speaker, Retreat Leader, Corporate Trainer/Consultant, and Business Development Coach.*

- *He writes extensively on the topics of Personal, Professional and Spiritual Development, with a focus on Selling, CRM, and Personal Communication Skills.*
- *He speaks from the heart with passion and humor: A proud recipient of prestigious recognition, such as Salesman of the Year, Toastmaster of the Year, Speaker of the Year, and Toronto Member of the Year for the Canadian Association of Professional Speakers.*
- *Specializing in communication competencies: Professional Selling, Creative Customer Care (CRM), Presentation and Facilitation Skills, Phone Skills, Technology, Business Writing, Writing for Sales, Marketing and Ad Copy, Speech Writing, Educational and Courseware Materials Development, Effective Coaching and Motivation Skills, and Public Speaking Mastery.*

• How I Got Started

IT'S GOOD TO REFLECT

Contemplation helps remind us how far we've come in our life journey; in my case, the journey crossed great social and economic distances. I've enjoyed a life filled with incredible experiences; challenges, blessings and triumph in many areas of personal, spiritual, as well as professional development.

I STAND BY MY VISIONS

The first memorable vision was quite bizarre, yet was delivered to me with amazing clarity at just ten years old. We were living in New York State. I remember standing on the steps of our big front porch. I even remember the address written on the green post at 68 Oliver Street.

In *The Magic of Thinking BIG*, author Dr. David Schwartz says that when we choose to believe in our desired reality, we'll actually make it happen.

The vision lasted only a few seconds, but was complete, detailed and meant absolutely nothing to me at that time. Let me explain, I am the son of many generations of blue-collar working stiffs who would never knowingly come into contact with business people, let alone professional speakers or consultants.

In that vision, I was on a raised platform in front of a great crowd pressing in. They appeared to be eagerly waiting for information; they seemed happy—not hostile, and the weirdest thing of all, their hands were held out towards me, clinching money. Weird—why would anyone ever pay another person for information?

Today, as a professional speaker, I would kill for such a cash laden audience, but as a ten year old, the vision held no value, and it left me as fast as it came. How could I have appreciated the significance of that "moment of truth" in my young life, especially since my friends were waiting to do some serious exploring on our bicycles that afternoon?

AT SOME POINT, WE MUST BUY-IN TO OUR DREAMS

Nine years later, the truth of the earlier vision thumped me and I became a willing participant in my life's ultimate destiny.

By age 19, I was determined to become the one to change our family's work experience legacy by trying my hand at selling. I loved cars and figured out that they also brought the possibility of a better social life, so I became a car salesman in the mid 1970s, mainly because I couldn't afford a car or a girlfriend for that matter. I considered myself a young hotshot with something to prove. A top producer right away, I earned recognition as a Senior Salesmaster during my second year.

People buy People—products and services just come with the package. Theriault Life Discoveries

---

During this time period, the next vision came to me while I was sitting in Toronto's famous old Massy Hall with about one thousand other wannabe sales greats. I was about to witness my first motivational speaker; actually, for me, the first live speaker of any kind. Zig Ziglar delivered 17 words that changed my life forever and have served me well to this day. "You'll get what you want out of life after you've helped enough others get what they want." I don't know why his message meant so much to me, but it did. I guess my subconscious mind regarded his words as a lifeline, and clung to them as if both success and survival depended on it.

My willpower became engaged that day in the form of a BIG personal goal. Something birthed in my soul; I saw myself on stage with Zig, doing what he does. I can't explain it. It just made sense to me that my destiny-by-design would be to serve through speaking. But what did I have to speak about? My resolve was to work hard for twenty years. Since most people worked for forty years before retiring, I vowed to cut that time in half—and then live to tell about it.

Leadership development expert Dr. John Maxwell says, "See it—Say it—Seize it" in his popular self-help book *BE All YOU CAN BE!*

I promised, I'd sell everything and anything I could find; I'll gain firsthand experience in different industries; I'll be known as an expert in personal communication, all the while creating the substance and style of my future motivational speeches.

LIVING YOUR DREAMS IS UP TO YOU

I realized my twenty-year goal one full year ahead of schedule. While that's a great story about a know-nothing rough-around-the-edges guy in his late teens, my success hides a somber truth. The truth is I was in control of my life all along, but I didn't know it. I just took a guess and it worked. Thanks Zig.

• My Biggest Mistake

My biggest lifetime mistake was not having enough faith in myself earlier. Since then, I've discovered that faith is free, a renewable resource, so feel free to lay claim to all you can get.

Therefore today, my strongest message of encouragement is don't make the same mistake I did. I could have chosen to take only ten years or just five for the journey. The choice really was mine, but my lack of self-confidence at 19 caused me to believe my destination would take twenty years. And since our actions are always dictated by our beliefs, it took about twenty years.

You see I didn't "feel worthy" of greatness. I had no one to tell me, "You can make it; you can become whatever you want to be, just believe in yourself and work to your desired end." But I wanted it badly anyway, so I took a chance. I picked a goal, stayed positive and became a passionate pursuer of a dream. Now that I know a journey will take whatever time we allow it, I spend my time encouraging others to stop thinking about it and just go for it.

You'll get what you want out of life after you've helped enough others get what they want.

Zig Ziglar

Allow me to share this thought. Tell yourself that today you'll start thinking differently; you'll believe in you and make all future predictions with your ultimate destiny in mind. Then you will become a willing participant; the designer of your life's journey. Your special destiny awaits your arrival. It will allow you to take your time, but don't. Get there as fast as you can!

• My Best Success

Many of us struggle with the concepts of worth and value. Like the old saying, I believe that beauty really is "in the eye of the beholder." One of the most important, and therefore most profitable lessons I've learned in the meetings industry is it's also true that "value is in the mind of the beholder."

I learned this truth by accident when, during the initial interview, a prospective client offered me an amount equal to twice my usual fee at that time. I didn't want to disappoint him by saying I'm not in that price range yet, so I took the assignment; went home and studied long and hard so that when the event date came, I would be worth every penny… and I was.

If you don't have what you want yet… go help some more people. Theriault Life Discoveries

---

If then, value is a byproduct of perception, worth resides solely in the mind of the presenter. When speaking about money and speaking fees, make every effort to fully understand your client's perceptions on the subject of value. But your worth? That's always been up to you. The following idea has immense value, but I always give it away just the same.

THE WORLD'S SHORTEST SALES SEMINAR

In over 25 years of selling, managing and training, I enjoy reducing concepts down to their base elements whenever possible.

It's true that the selling and buying process seems difficult to understand to most people, but I've come up with a comprehensive, simple explanation that anyone can grasp.

It employs only twelve words to express effectively, and this seminar takes just four seconds to deliver. Be forewarned that selling really is simple. Here it is…

"Everyone will buy once they realize what they'll loose if they don't."

• What I Would Do Over

I'd seek out more and better quality coaches earlier. These days "coaching" is the hottest buzzword, and rightly so. But a few years ago, managers worked hard at attempting to mold their people into preconceived, industry standards of behaviour and outdated performance models, which have little to do with productivity.

Today's wise managers understand the folly of their predecessors and elect to become effective at coaching and motivate through strong relationships, which fosters the ideas of personal accountability, high performance teams and brand loyalty.

If I were given a chance to do it over, to get it right so to speak, I'd do what I'm doing today—find as many good quality coaches as possible and become a dedicated student of their wisdom; becoming empowered by their encouragement.

1. I'd seek these individuals out in proven effective professional organizations like NSA (National Speakers Association in the U.S.), CAPS (Canadian Association of Professional Speakers) and Toastmasters International.

2. I'd find colleagues/friends who need the coaching that my life/work experiences could offer, in order to fully understand the impact of good coaching from both aspects or receiving and giving.

3. I'd focus only on the BIG stuff of life and work, and let the small stuff slip away into obscurity where it belongs. I'd read, *Don't Sweat the Small Stuff* by Richard Carlson PhD (Hyperion) and *The Prayer of Jabez* by Dr. Bruce Wilkinson (Multnomah) before ever being concerned about crucial business acumen, such as process and product knowledge and company policy.

My dominant life-conclusion thus far is that by concentrating on creating a better person, you automatically get a better (assured, peaceful and effective) employee, boss, spouse or friend. We really are in control of our individual destiny and our socially shared results!

CAPS

PROFESSIONAL TRAINERS,
FACILITATORS AND KEYNOTERS

George Torok

George Torok Seminars

Phone: 905-631-0595
E-mail: George@Torok.com
Web: **www.Torok.com**

GEORGE TOROK *is co-author of the national best seller,* Secrets of Power Marketing—*Canada's first guide to personal marketing. The book is published in seven countries.*

Torok is the host of the weekly radio show 'Business in Motion' on 93.3 CFMU. He interviews leaders and innovators from business, community and associations.

After more than 20 years in corporate management he launched his own successful business delivering motivational keynotes and practical seminars across North America. He specializes in helping professionals, executives and leaders with their thinking and communication skills. He offers personal coaching and specialized consulting. He delivers keynote speeches and training programs in Personal Marketing, Presentation Skills and Creative Problem Solving.

George Torok links people with information, ideas and skills. Audiences remark on his relevance, warmth and infectious enthusiasm. Often called upon as a marketing guru, he was featured in the media as a Citizen of the World.

• How I Got Started

Before entering the world of entrepreneurship, my last employer was the Ontario government. One of my roles I enjoyed was presenting to committees and speaking at meetings all over the province. Fortunately, I did two things to upgrade my communication skills. I hired a tutor for writing and attended a two-day course on presentation skills. From the writing tutor I learned about organizing, structure and most importantly discovered the concept of *tone*. With my new understanding, the material I had previously written, I read with great embarrassment.

There is nothing in a caterpillar that tells you it's going to be a butterfly. Buckminster Fuller

---

From the presentation skills course, I experienced two career-defining revelations. One, I was not as good a presenter as I thought. Two, there was a system of presentation techniques that I could learn, practise and hone.

The confidence I gained from that seminar encouraged me to volunteer to chair the annual conference of my association. I got to hire the speakers. As conference chair I got to make several short speeches—you know—"Welcome!" and "The washrooms are down the hall," and "Have a safe trip home."

Show me the names on your database and I know who you are. Peter Urs Bender

---

At the conclusion of that conference I was ecstatic. I called Fraser McCallum and Arabella Bengson, who had delivered that pivotal presentations skills seminar. I announced, "I want to do this for a living."

They chuckled, and then dispensed four key bits of advice: 1. Don't quit your day job yet. 2. Join Toastmasters to get good at the craft. 3. Speak anywhere to anybody for anything—for the practice and to build a reputation. 4. Over time, focus on becoming known as an expert. I followed their advice and it worked. Thank you Arabella and Fraser!

• My Biggest Mistake

No one mistake stands out in my memory. That means one of two things. Either it was so bad I erased it from memory or I did not take enough risks to make the big mistakes. I choose to believe the second reason. In that case, my biggest mistake may be forgettable because it was an error of omission not commission. I needed to push harder, sooner and more often.

I made and continue to make mistakes I am certain. I learn from them and move on.

• My Best Success

My best success came from a few areas…. From attending the meetings, workshops and conventions I learned the business inside out. Participating in CAPS and NSA was where I learned the speaking business and all of its manifestations. I discovered there is no one correct formula although there are formulas you can adapt for your success.

You cannot take a course on how to become a successful professional speaker. That is why there is CAPS. I am reminded of my back packing world travels as a youth. Wherever I traveled, I always met someone who had just left where I was going. CAPS is the same way. You can always find someone who has been there or is heading in the same direction. Everything else started through CAPS—ideas, connections and example.

MY MENTOR AND FRIEND PETER URS BENDER, CSP., HOF

Peter taught me many insights about his success. He encouraged me to grow and to write my first book. Peter fed me with his advice, example and inspiration. He opened doors for me—some by introduction and others by association. We wrote a book together and continue to work together on some projects.

He who asks is a fool for five minutes but he who does not ask remains a fool forever. Chinese Proverb

---

I did not specifically look for a mentor. I did seek out successful people in the field I entered to learn from them. I was lucky that one of the *greats* took a shine to me. If you are lucky you may find a mentor. Remember that no one owes you anything. If you go out of your way to meet successful people, someone may take you under their wing and mentor you for an hour, month, or perhaps a year.

WRITING MY BOOK, "SECRETS OF POWER MARKETING"

Publishing my book positioned me as an (the?) expert. It redefined my business. The best thing you can do to catapult your speaking business is to write. Write articles. And especially, write a book. Although not the same skill sets, writing and speaking do complement. Being in print boosts your credibility more than speaking.

Where your talents and the world's needs cross, there lies your vocation. Aristotle

---

HOSTING MY RADIO SHOW, "BUSINESS IN MOTION"

I interview corporate executives, community leaders and innovators. The radio show taught me self-confidence. In the beginning I felt intimidated by some of my very powerful guests. They did not intimidate me—but I let myself be intimidated by them until I realized that I could not be them—but I was good at being me. Within those boundaries, we were equal. Once I learned to treat them as my equals, they treated me accordingly.

Hosting a radio show opened many doors to executives and key contacts. The idea came to me while I was interviewed as a guest on the radio show of another CAPS member, Jim Harris. Sitting in the studio, I gazed around and exclaimed to myself, "I can do this." My show has been running for more than six years—and I love it. An added benefit is the development of my interviewing and listening skills.

Strong relationships with your clients and prospects will earn you more business than price and quality alone. George Torok

---

My show is with a community radio station at McMaster University. Most colleges and universities have a community radio station. They are starved for good talk show hosts. You do not have to be a student or graduate of that school to host a show.

• What I Would Do Over

If I had it all to do over again, knowing then what I know now, I would:

• Do more and sooner.

• Take bigger risks so I could learn faster. Success in this business comes from acting boldly.

• Develop products sooner.

• Contract out some tasks.

Even though I would do more I would also take the advice of past national CAPS president, Patricia Katz, and "pause more."

We're overpaying him but he's worth it.

Samuel Goldwin

Quotes

The greatest achievement of the human spirit is to live up to one's opportunities and make the most of one's resources.

—Marquis De Vauvenargues (p. 25)

I dread success. To have succeeded is to have finished one's business on earth, like the male spider, who is killed by the female the moment he has succeeded in courtship. I like a state of continual becoming, with a goal in front and not behind.

—George Bernard Shaw (p. 26)

A life spent making mistakes is not only more honorable, but more useful than a life spent doing nothing.

—George Bernard Shaw (p. 27)

Courage is fear that has said its prayers.

—Karle Wilson Baker (p. 28)

I have learned that success is to be measured not so much by the position that one has reached in life as by the obstacles which he has overcome while trying to succeed.

—Booker T. Washington (p.28)

Your past was perfect to get you where you are today.

—Peter Urs Bender (p. 31)

If we do what we always done, we get what we always gotten.

—Peter Urs Bender (p. 32)

You cannot—not market.

—Peter Urs Bender (p. 33)

The smarter I work, the luckier I get.

—Peter Urs Bender (p. 34)

Do not read your speech—read your audience.

—Peter Urs Bender (p. 34)

Nothing great was ever achieved without enthusiasm.

—Emerson (p. 37)

The brighter you are, the more you have to learn.

—Ralph Waldo Emerson (p. 38)

It matters not how long we live, but how.

—Bailey (p. 39)

Many receive advice, only the wise profit by it.

—Syrus (p. 40)

No person should part with their individuality and become that of another.

—Channing (p. 41)

Nothing is so contagious as enthusiasm; it moves stones, it tames brutes. Enthusiasm is the genius of sincerity and truth accomplishes no victories without it.

—Bulwer-Lytton (p. 42)

Only you can do it, but you don't have to do it alone.

—Brian Dalzell (p. 45)

Trees can't run, Rocks can't fly and Rivers just flow without purpose. People do the best they can with what they have and who they are.

—Brian Dalzell (p. 46)

Fear is the gatekeeper to our new realities.

—Brian Dalzell (p. 47)

Beliefs are like Boxes. We can either build Barriers or Bridges.

—Brian Dalzell (p. 48)

Our biggest gains in learning come from our greatest losses in life.

—Brian Dalzell (p. 48)

Speak to me from the heart; I'll use mine to listen.

—Peter de Jager (p. 51)

The tallest mountains lean up against the deepest valleys.

—Peter de Jager (p. 52)

The experience of others is knowledge awaiting harvest.

—Peter de Jager (p. 53)

You got great promotional material; it's word of mouth that's killing you.

—The CAPS Pool PEG (p. 57)

You can't get all the money this year; that's why they call it a career

—Don Kyle (p. 58)

You decide when you stop speaking; they decide when the presentation is over.

—Warren Evans (p. 59)

You can't luck into repeat business.

—Anonymous (p. 60)

One big marketing challenge that distinguishes this business is that most products don't have ego's.

—Warren Evans (p. 61)

There are lot's of people in your life who need to change, start with yourself.

—Peggy Grall (p. 65)

If you want it perfect—don't do it live.

—Unknown (p. 66)

If you're not living on the edge, you're taking up too much room.

—African Proverb (p. 67)

Our deepest fear is not that we are inadequate. Our deepest fear is that we are powerful beyond measure. It is our light, not our darkness, than most frightens us. We ask ourselves, Who am I to be brilliant, gorgeous, talented, fabulous? Actually, who are you not to be?

—Marianne Williamson (p. 68)

People will forget what you said. People will forget what you did, but people will never forget how you made them feel.

—Unknown (p. 69)

There are many things in life that will catch your eye, but only a few will catch your heart… pursue those.

—Unknown (p. 70)

The effectiveness of our memory banks is determined not by the total number of facts we take in, but the number we wish to reject.

—Jon Wynne-Tyson (p. 73)

You are told a lot about your education, but some beautiful, sacred memory, preserved since childhood, is perhaps the best education of all. If a man carries many such memories into life with him, he is saved for the rest of his days. And even if only one good memory is left in our hearts, it may also be the instrument of our salvation one day.

—Fyodor Dostoevski (p. 74)

The true art of memory is the art of attention.

—Samuel Johnson (p. 75)

The charm, one might say the genius of memory, is that it is choosy, chancy, and temperamental: it rejects the edifying cathedral and indelibly photographs the small boy outside, chewing a hunk of melon in the dust.

—Elizabeth Bowen (p. 76)

Do what you can, with what you have, where you are.

—Theodore Roosevelt (p. 79)

Write it on your heart that every day is the best day of the year.

—Ralph Waldo Emerson (p. 80)

Sharing what you have is more important than what you have.

—Albert M. Wells, Jr. (p. 80)

Nothing is impossible to a willing heart.

—John Heywood (p. 81)

When you have learned to love, you have learned to live.

—Angela Jackson (p. 82)

Good company in a journey makes the way seem shorter.

—Izaak Walton (p. 83)

Get out of your house. Get out of your head.

—Kelly McCormick (p. 85)

Risking is moving past your acceptable limits.

—Unknown (p. 87)

It's not always about the speaker. It's about the audience.

—MG (p. 87)

Just go for it kid.

—Bob (Dad) McCormick (p.88)

Some things turn me on, as if I'd swallowed a neon sign.

—Smoke Blanchard (p. 91)

Astound me. Try your hardest. These last flashes of astonishment are what I cannot live without.

—Colette, Earthly Paradise (p. 92)

Nature loves to hide. It rests by changing.

—Heraclitus (p. 94)

Everybody loves something, even if it's only tortillas.

—T. Rinpoche (p. 95)

Success must be a shared experience.

—Mary Kay Ash (p. 97)

You never achieve real success unless you like what you are doing.

—Dale Carnegie (p. 98)

Success… is connecting with the audience.

—Rosalie Moscoe (p. 99)

Education will never become as expensive as ignorance.

—Unknown (p. 100)

Sometimes we have to risk it.

—Reva Nelson (p. 101)

I am a great believer in luck, and I find the harder I work, the more I have of it.

—Stephen Leacock (p.103)

I never did a day's work in my life—it was all fun.

—Thomas Alva Edison (p. 104)

The tongue is the only tool that gets sharper with use.

—Anonymous (p. 105)

There is nothing wrong with having nothing to say, unless you insist on saying it.

—Anonymous (p. 106)

Character is determined by what you accomplish when the excitement is gone.

—Anonymous (p. 107)

Life is a dance partner waiting for us to take the first step; then lead with passion and joy.

—Reva Nelson (p. 110)

To know, trust and act from your own truth is the most essential risk of all.

—Reva Nelson (p. 110)

There is no grief which time does not lessen or soften.

—Cicero (p. 112)

The ultimate lesson which all of us have to learn is unconditional love, which includes not only others but ourselves as well.

—Elisabeth Kübler-Ross (p. 113)

In any initiative or opportunity pursuit there is an element of risk.

—Edward de Bono (p. 114)

What I do today is important, for I am paying a day of my life for it. What I accomplish must be worthwhile, for the price is high.

—Unknown (p.117)

Think like a man of action, act like a man of thought.

—Henri Bergson (p. 118)

The significant problems we have cannot be solved at the same level of thinking with which we created them.

—Albert Einstein (p. 119)

The most erroneous stories are those we think we know best—and therefore never scrutinize or question.

—Stephen Jay Gould (p. 119)

If you think you can do a thing or think you can't do a thing, you're right.

—Henry Ford (p. 120)

Take time to deliberate, but when the time for action has arrived, stop thinking and go in.

—Napoleon Bonaparte (p. 120)

If you would lift me, you must be on higher ground.

—Ralph Waldo Emerson (p. 123)

It is okay to stumble because you are moving forward.

—Anonymous (p. 124)

Never insult an alligator until you have crossed the river.

—Cordell Hull (p. 125)

I respect faith, but doubt is what gives you an education.

—Wilson Mizner (p. 126)

True marketing doesn't ask what you want to sell, but what the customer wants to buy.

—Peter Drucker (p. 126)

When you win, nothing hurts.

—Joe Namath (p. 127)

The trials and tribulations of life bring each of us our share of disappointments. Yet, they also leave behind a greater sense of understanding, toleration and sympathy for others— something we never felt to the same extent when we were younger.

—Marianne Williamson (p. 127)

Preparedness: Be prepared to expand on a presentation point when the audience reaction is positive for greater impact and to demonstrate your natural expertise in the subject.

—Richard Peterson (p. 129)

Simplicity in Visuals: Carefully chosen, easy to read visuals will show your audience advance planning, creativity and thinking that weaves its way throughout your presentation.

—Richard Peterson (p. 131)

Influential Finish: Your powerful final words may be the most remembered; the finish will hold more influence with the audience if met with conclusion moving to timely action.

—Richard Peterson (p. 133)

When you follow your bliss... doors will open where you would not have thought there would be doors; and where there wouldn't be a door for anyone else.

—Joseph Campbell (p. 135)

Failure is only the opportunity to begin again more intelligently.

—Henry Ford (p. 136)

Communication is more than a sharing of words. It is the wise sharing of emotions, feelings, and concerns. It is the sharing of oneself totally.

—Marvin J. Ashton (p.137)

Sometimes we get stuck with "three to get ready, three to get ready"

—Rosita Perez (p. 138)

It's never too late to become what you might have been.

—George Elliot (p. 141)

There are no mistakes, no coincidences, all events are blessings given to us to learn from.

—Elizabeth Kübler-Ross (p. 142)

When one is a stranger to oneself, then one is estranged from others too.

—Anne Morrow Lindburgh (p. 143**)**

We don't see things as they are, we see them as we are.

—Anaïs Nin (p. 144)

Without information you cannot take responsibility; with information you can't avoid it.

—Jan Carlzon (p. 145)

The shoemaker makes a good shoe because he makes nothing else.

—Emerson (p. 147)

Some folks are wise and some are otherwise.

—Tobias George Smollet (p. 148)

Don't tell me I can't do it. Tell me what I need to do to make it happen.

—Tom Stoyan (p. 149)

Every person is the architect of their own fortune.

—English Proverb (p. 150)

One of the difficulties in bringing about change in an organization is that you must do so through the persons who have been most successful in that organization, no matter how faulty the system or organization is. To such persons, you see, it is the best of all possible organizations because look who was selected by it and look who succeeded most with it. Yet, these are the very people through whom we must bring about improvements.

—George Washington (p. 152)

Does all this change make people feel insecure? Of course. But anybody who recognizes what is going on in this world and isn't somewhat insecure, I would argue, is not awake. And I think the biggest enemy of progress is happy talk. You need to tell people that if we do not change, and change fundamentally,

we are going out of business. And that will create insecurity.
The trick is to turn that insecurity into constructive tension.

—Mike Walsh, former CEO, Tenneco, (p. 154)

It's hard to plot a rational course in an irrational environment. So don' t be blinded by reason or logic. Be ever vigilant. Take a nap and you could wake up like Rip Van Winkle!

—Watts Wacker, The 500 Year Delta, (p. 156)

In order for an organization to succeed, it must be resilient, flexible and selective in an unpredictable world, and its planners must be intelligent, visionary and brave.

—R.E. Wilhelm, EXXON, (p. 156)

Prepare for eternity: Tidy up your room.

—Ashleigh Brilliant (p. 157)

Motivation and inspiration make difficult things seem more possible. Action makes them happen!

—Linda Tarrant (p. 157)

Wise men talk because they have something to say; fools because they have to say something.

—Plato (p. 161)

When we choose to believe in our desired reality, we'll actually make it happen.

—Dr. David Schwartz (p. 165)

People buy People—products and services just come with the package.

—Theriault Life Discoveries (p. 166)

"See it—Say it—Seize it"

—Dr. John Maxwell (p. 167)

"You'll get what you want out of life after you've helped enough others get what they want."

—Zig Ziglar (p. 168)

"If you don't have what you want yet… go help some more people."

—Theriault Life Discoveries (p. 169)

There is nothing in a caterpillar that tells you it's going to be a butterfly.

—Buckminster Fuller (p. 173)

Show me the names on your database and I know who you are.

—Peter Urs Bender (p. 173)

He who asks is a fool for five minutes but he who does not ask remains a fool forever.

—Chinese Proverb (p. 175)

Where your talents and the world's needs cross, there lies your vocation.

—Aristotle (p. 175)

Strong relationships with your clients and prospects will earn you more business than price and quality alone.

—George Torok (p. 176)

We're overpaying him but he's worth it.

—Samuel Goldwin (p. 177)

List of Authors & Topic of Expertise

The information in this resource section was current at the time of publication. However, we cannot guarantee that changes haven't occurred since then. Please note that you should always confirm important information and act accordingly.

You are encouraged to use the information to your fullest advantage, as part of your ongoing search for new ways to improve your speaking competency and consequently, your business or career. We wish you: Graceful speaking and grateful audiences!

ARMSTRONG, SUSAN
(For contact information, see page 24)

Communication • Customer Service • Personal Development • Sales • Sales Management • Training

BENDER, PETER URS
(For contact information, see page 30)

Business Management • Communication • Leadership • Motivation • Presentation Skills • Sales

THORNLEY-BROWN, ANNE
(For contact information, see page 36)

Change •Creativity • Life Balance • Media • Spirituality• Teambuilding

DALZELL, BRIAN
(For contact information, see page 44)

Business Management • Change • Inspiration • Spirituality • Sales • Strategic Development

DE JAGER, PETER
(For contact information, see page 50)

Change • Computer/Internet • E-Business/E-Commerce • Future Trends

EVANS, WARREN
(For contact information, see page 56)

Future Trends • Leadership

GRALL, PEGGY
(For contact information, see page 64)

Business Management, • Change • Communication • Health/Wellness • Leadership • Personal Effectiveness • Teambuilding

GRAY, BOB
(For contact information, see page 72)

Customer Service • Humour • Memory • Personal Development • Personal Effectiveness • Sales

JACKSON, ANGELA
(For contact information, see page 78)

Communication • Inspiration • Leadership • Personal Effectiveness • Spirituality • Stress

MCCORMICK, KELLY
(For contact information, see page 84)

Communication • Leadership • Personal Effectiveness •Problem Solving • Teambuilding

MILNE, MAGGIE
(For contact information, see page 90)

Creativity • Human Resource • Strategic Development

MOSCOE, ROSALIE
(For contact information, see page 96)

Health/Wellness • Image/Self-Esteem • Personal Development • Stress • Time/Self Management

NATH, SUNJAY
(For contact information, see page 102)

Family/Youth • Motivation • Presentation Skills • Teambuilding • Time/Self Management

NELSON, REVA
(For contact information, see page 108)

Change • Consulting • Inspiration • Leadership • Personal Effectiveness • Presentation Skills

PARK, RANDY
(For contact information, see page 116)

Communication • Computer/Internet • Leadership • Personal Effectiveness • Strategic Development • Technology

PAULSEN, TIM
(For contact information, see page 122)

Communication • Customer Service • Finance • Stress • Time/Self Management • Training

PETERSON, RICHARD
(For contact information, see page 128)

Communication • Humour • Negotiating • Presentation Skills • Sales • Sales Management

SAUNDERSON, ROY
(For contact information, see page 134)

Empowerment • Human Resource • Image/Self-Esteem • Leadership • Motivation • Success

SINDEN, JEAN
(For contact information, see page 140)

Business Management • Change • Entrepreneurship • Leadership • Personal Effectiveness • Strategic Development

STOYAN, TOM
(For more contact information, see page 146)

Sales

TARRANT, LINDA
(For contact information, see page 152)

Change • Creativity • Leadership • Motivation • Teambuilding

TAYLOR, HAROLD
(For contact information, see page 158)

Personal Effectiveness • Stress • Time/Self Management

THERIAULT, FRANCIS
(For contact information, see page 164)

Communication • Customer Service • Motivation • Personal Development • Spirituality • Sales

TOROK, GEORGE
(For contact information, see page 172)

Creativity • Leadership • Marketing • Presentation Skills • Problem Solving

a nationally broadcasted CBC news magazine show geared to towards teenagers called "From the Hip". He also worked as a reporter for an educational news program before becoming a writer/producer for a local news outlet. He followed that with a five-year stint in the advertising field, working as an account manager, helping execute the marketing plan for the country's largest sporting goods retailer.

After penning thousands of news stories, a stack of sporting goods catalogues and a dozen installments of his now famous annual Christmas letter – this is Gregory's very first crack at writing a book.

AUTHOR BIO

Gregory Tysowski is a certified expert at the stay-at-home dad position. Starting his new gig in the fall of 2003, his career as homemaker really took off in 2005. That's when his responsibilities doubled as he juggled two kids under the age of two, tried to stay on top of the laundry and slow-cooked his way into the rank of top chef. Greg-ory has been married for over twenty years to his lovely wife, Lianne, and has two children, Abigail and Daniel. Prior to his success on the home front, Gregory received his English degree from the University of Saskatchewan in 1991, and followed that up with a degree in Journalism & Communications from the University of Regina in 1993.

Gregory specialized in Broadcast Journalism, and has worked several jobs in the media busi-ness. He started his career as a field producer for

And just one more thing.

If my son ever mentions to me again that he wants to be a stay-at-home dad when he grows up, I'll be sure to tell him that nothing in this world would make me prouder.

FINI

✳ ✳

In the past twelve years, I have had a front row seat for everything and anything that has even come close to being considered a milestone - first tooth, first words, first wobbly baby steps, first boo-boo, first projectile vomit, first day of school, first eye-roll and more. You name it; I was there for it. I'll still be there for the next round of firsts - first acne break-out, first love, first broken heart, first "I hate you, Dad" - and I swear that I will try to cherish every minute of it all. I've experienced something that very few men ever will, and I'm extremely proud of that.

When our first child was born, so was the idea to author this book. It took me over ten years to finally get off my ass and start writing it. And, by my calculations, we have a little under ten more years before we can punt our second born child out of the house and begin life as empty nesters. If the next decade of parenthood is as eventful as the first, I'll be in for more life-altering adventures and will accumulate plenty of fresh fodder for my second masterpiece, the inevitable sequel to this first testament of my stay-at-home chronicles. If I were smart and organized, I would start planning by taking notes now of the entertaining episodes that life brings me instead of waiting until the last minute. Oh, who am I kidding? I'll just play it by ear all over again and see what happens. That's how I roll.